FINDING
SAVOONGA

LETTERS FROM THE EDGE OF AMERICA

Dear mother, we experienced a rare occurrence that we shall never forget,,,

Doris D. Ray

FINDING SAVOONGA
Letters from the Edge of America

Published by Gatekeeper Press
2167 Stringtown Rd., Suite 109
Columbus, OH 43123-2989
www.GatekeeperPress.com
The cover design, interior formatting, typesetting, and editorial work for this book
are entirely the product of the author. Gatekeeper Press did not participate in this work
and is not responsible for any aspect of it.

Publication management: Kent Sturgis Publishing Services, LLC
Editor: Kent Sturgis
Researcher: Karen Cedzo
Proofreader: Patricia Sturgis
Design: Elizabeth Watson, Watson Graphics
Colorization: William Campbell, Mars Premedia
Map: Kroll Map Co.

For more information, contact Doris D. Ray at ckddray@comcast.net.

Photo credits: Except for the photo on page 22 of fishing on the Columbia River, which is
published courtesy of the U.S. Army Corps of Engineers, all photos herein are drawn from the
private collection of Doris D. Ray. The photos on pages 42, 76, 87, 88, 103, and 208 have been
colorized from original black and white prints.

Other photos: front cover – A musher and his dogsled team return home at dusk with a
piece of lumber scavenged from the sea; back cover – Julia Alowa, Nellie Seppilu and Jenny
Alowa pose for a photo near the school; title page (page 2) – Doris Ray enjoys an exhilarating
skinboat ride from Gambell to Savoonga.

Note to readers: Some of the letters in *Finding Savoonga* have been edited for length, clarity,
and best organization in book form.

Library of Congress Control Number: 2023935793

ISBN: 978-1-6629-3613-5 (paperback)
e-ISBN: 978-1-6629-3614-2

*For Tod, who shared these
and many other adventures in our
more than 68 years of marriage.
With love.*

▲ *Letters from the edge of America.*

PAGE 10

PAGE 76

PAGE 178

Dear John, Charles + Jimmie,

We are still impatiently waiting for another letter from you. Grandma has kept us up to date on all your activities while she was here, but we haven't heard from you for quite a while.

We often think it would be so nice if you boys could come up to visit us next summer. You would have so much fun with the Eskimo children. Most of them know enough English to be understood. One little boy named Gabriel, who is about 10 years old, made me a beautiful paper weight for Xmas. He does very good carving for a boy so young and I was very pleased to have it.

We have been having a fine time up here. Uncle Tod plans to go walrus hunting with some of the men now that the Ice is a Leary parka —

Well, we must hurry over to the post office to mail all our letters, as there are some dog sleds leaving tomorrow for Gambell — write us soon.

Love
Aunt Dais + Uncle Tod

▲ *Tod and I mailed letters from Savoonga, Alaska, weather permitting.*

Preface

❖ ❖ ❖

While sorting through my mother's belongings after her death, I discovered a cache of typed and hand-written letters I had written to her when my husband Charles (better known as Tod, his nickname) and I taught school from 1951 to 1954 in a remote Yupik village on St. Lawrence Island in the northern Bering Sea off the Alaska coast.

I took the letters home and tossed them into a drawer where they remained for decades. A similar collection of letters was found in my sister-in-law's belongings after her death. We laid claim to them, and they, too, went into the drawer—to be looked at later. Years passed.

One evening in late 2020, several months after my husband's death, I was visiting with close friends **Nancy** and **Neil McReynolds**. The subject of family reminiscences came up, and I mentioned the old letters from St. Lawrence Island. Having visited the island, Neil was interested in our experience. He urged me to do something with the letters, possibly publish them, as they described life in a long-gone pre-industrial hunting society.

I wasn't enthusiastic. However, the Covid epidemic was raging, we were quarantined, and my daily activities were increasingly limited. So, I decided, if nothing else, I would type the letters into a document file so that I might reread and remember what I had written. Many months later, the letters were in the computer.

After organizing them into chapters, I wondered if they should be published. I needed the advice of an old friend, **Kent Sturgis**, whom I had known as a student when I was a teacher at Lathrop High School in Fairbanks in the 1960s. Kent had been professionally involved in publishing in Seattle. I knew his expertise and advice would be invaluable. However, I was unable to locate his telephone number or email address.

I mentioned my dilemma in a 2021 holiday letter to **Bruce Heflinger** and his wife **Mary**. Bruce was another student who became a life-long friend. The next thing I knew, I was having a telephone conversation with **Alan Wilken**, another good friend, former student, and member of the Lathrop High School "old boys' network." Bruce had contacted Alan, who knew how to contact Kent. And with that information I was able to move forward.

A telephone reunion with Kent resulted in his agreement to edit the letters and arrange for possible publication. Indeed, without Kent's careful editing and suggestions that improved the manuscript, this project would not have come to fruition.

Jeff Cook, another dear friend and former student, emailed me regularly through the months of writing and rewriting to learn of my progress and offer his enthusiastic support.

Chery Cutler McHugh, yet another old friend from a Lathrop history classroom, offered her assistance. In one of her emails, she urged me to include an anecdote I'd shared with her class about ordering a year's supply of "cucumber chips," not realizing that I would be receiving immense quantities of dill pickles.

I thanked Chery for the reminder and revealed that I had NOT written my mother about the night I swore at the Presbyterian missionary. Mother would have written back, "My dear, I'm VERY DISAPPOINTED in you!"

However, it brought back that memorable evening many years ago.

We were in the habit of having dinner on Saturday nights with Alice Green, the missionary—one week at our place, the next up at the manse. After dinner, we played three-handed pinochle. In this game, as the cards are dealt, the dealer sets aside a three-card pot that players can bid on to improve their hands.

I had been dealt a hand with three of the four cards for a double pinochle. If I won the pot, and it contained the fourth card, I would be richer by some 300 points. So, I was bidding for the pot.

The missionary was bidding, too. Our bids went higher and higher. Finally, Alice said, "Bye," and I took the pot. Inside was my fourth card. A double pinochle! I let out a whoop. Then, Alice responded, "I didn't say 'bye'!"

"Well, goddamn!" I exploded. We were all shocked, me included. I *never* swore.

"I think we'll stop the game now," Tod said. And we did. This may have been the last time we played pinochle with Alice. I must say, though, that we remained friends with her over the years.

My nephew, **Jim Ashford**, and his wife **Pam** have followed this project from the beginning. Jim had received letters from Savoonga when he was a small lad and has been excited about the prospect of seeing them in print. He has called regularly with love and support.

Finally, my special friends at Horizon House, who listened to my presentations of book chapters on the Writers Read program, have earned my enduring gratitude for their encouragement and support. Thank you, dear friends.

Who's Who

THE FAMILIES

The caches of letters that gathered dust for years had been saved by our families in the Midwest. Rereading them for this book project brought back a flood of memories. Among the recipients were:

Addie Shepley Derby. A short, energetic, and affectionate woman, my mother was a beloved elementary school librarian in Detroit. She was prim and proper and always supported me in my educational goals. She enjoyed traveling extensively.

▲ My mother, Addie Derby, left, and Aunts Evelyn and Gladys "Glad."

Evelyn Shepley Hamill. My Aunt Evelyn, a motherly and nurturing caregiver, had been a high-school principal in Blind River, Ontario, before marrying a town doctor. Their son Bobbie was adopted when I was 14.

Gladys Shepley. My Aunt Gladys was a career librarian who headed the Windsor, Ontario, public library system. She was more of an older sister than aunt to me, despite the age difference. Gladys was always an empathetic listener who offered a haven in difficult times. She loved to travel, too.

The Ashfords

Eunice Ray Ashford. Tod's sister Eunice was 12 when Tod was born and assumed a role as his protector. Having a family of her own near Oklahoma City, Eunice remained especially close to Tod. She was an excellent cook and homemaker.

Herman Fillmore Ashford. Renamed "H.F." by Eunice at the beginning of their courtship,

▲ Eunice Ashford, left, Tod's sister, and her husband, Herman.

Tod's brother-in-law was a building contractor in the Oklahoma City area. I remember him as a tall, balding man who always wore a hat. He loved to fish with Tod during his summer visits to Colorado.

John and James Ashford. Tod's nephews were 9 and 7 years of age, respectively, in 1951. Exuberant, outgoing youngsters, they were popular in their neighborhood. They always looked forward to visits from Uncle Tod and Aunt Doris.

▲ *Tod's brother-in-law, Herman Fillmore ("H.F") Ashford, Tod, and two of Tod's nephews, Jimmie and John Ashford, in 1951.*

❖ ❖ ❖

THE VILLAGERS

Mentioned frequently in our letters were villagers who had helped us settle in to Savoonga and win acceptance in the village. Many became special friends, including:

Tim Gologergen. Tim, in his mid-to-late 30s, served as the teacher-aide in the school. An avid walrus and seal hunter who captained his own skinboat, he was also an officer in the Alaska National Guard and commanded the guard's Savoonga unit.

Amos Penayah. The school custodian until his retirement, Amos was a beloved and respected village elder who had been one of the first reindeer herders when reindeer were introduced on St. Lawrence Island.

▲ *Amos Penyah with sealskin floats.*

Albert Kulowiyi. Albert became school custodian when Amos retired. Ernest, thoughtful and dependable, Albert was a middle-aged church elder who greatly enjoyed attending Presbyterian Church conferences in the "Lower 48" states. Albert became a valued friend.

Ora Gologergen. Our second housekeeper and Tim's sister-in-law, Ora was a friendly, industrious woman who cared for a large family. She was particularly adept at skinning and preserving meat from animals her husband killed.

Ruth Miklahook. Ruth, our first housekeeper, provided much extra help including baking bread and darning clothes. She was a friendly, gregarious woman who loved to gossip, but the stories she told about her neighbors in the village were not always appreciated.

John Waghiyi. A quiet, industrious man in his mid-30s, John was an outstanding postmaster, a demanding position made difficult by irregular mail deliveries caused by bad weather and unreliable plane schedules. He and his wife Della had three small children.

Joseph Noongwook. Joseph carried mail between Gambell and Savoonga by dogsled or skinboat, depending on the season, fulfilling a time-consuming and sometimes dangerous responsibility with self-confidence. Joseph's wife, Katherine, became a close friend.

Theodore Kingeekuk. A quiet, kindly man, Theodore was one of Savoonga's most artful ivory-carvers, a skill he learned from his father and passed on to his older sons.

▲ Albert Kulowiyi

▲ Ruth Miklahook

▲ Theodore Kingeekuk

Mae Kingeekuk. A short, round woman in her 40s, Mae was skilled in sewing both cloth and skins. She instructed her daughters Janet and Della (Waghiyi) well in needlework.

Clarence Pungowiyi. A hunter and skinboat captain, Clarence was a friendly, loquacious storyteller who enjoyed visiting and passing along current and long-ago village anecdotes. His wife Helen was a quiet but friendly woman whom I often enjoyed visiting with as she sewed.

▲ *Mae Kingeekuk*

▲ *Helen Pungowiyi (back row, third from left) and husband Clarence (far right) and their family.*

Jacob Seppilu. The astute and competent manager of the native co-op store, Jacob bought arctic fox skins and ivory carvings for resale. He sold everything from vital supplies such as oil and kerosene to a modest selection of food and sewing supplies. His wife Myra, a good friend, managed a large family.

▲ *Jacob Seppilu*

▲ *Jimmie and Mabel Toolie with their children, Eugene, Gregory, and Ellen.*

Jimmie Toolie. A cheerful, fun-loving man, Jimmie might have been an Irish
leprechaun in another life. He and his crew were skilled hunters of walruses
and seals. His wife Mabel was a warm, motherly woman widely admired for
the beauty of her hand-made skin products such as *mukluks*.

Jonathan Annogiyuk. A friendly, outgoing young man who was an avid hunter
and trapper, Jonathan was exceedingly knowledgeable about the terrain of St.
Lawrence Island.

▲ *Jonathan Annogiyuk and friends.*

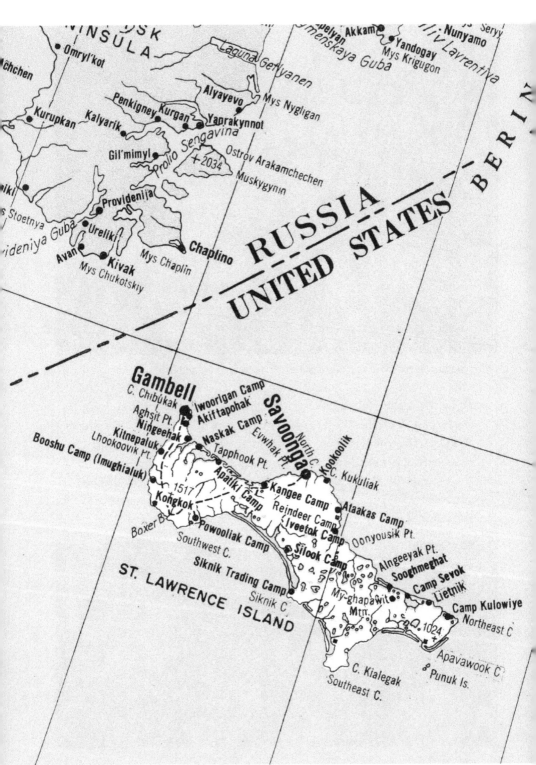

▲ *St. Lawrence Island is closer to Siberia than to the Alaska mainland.*

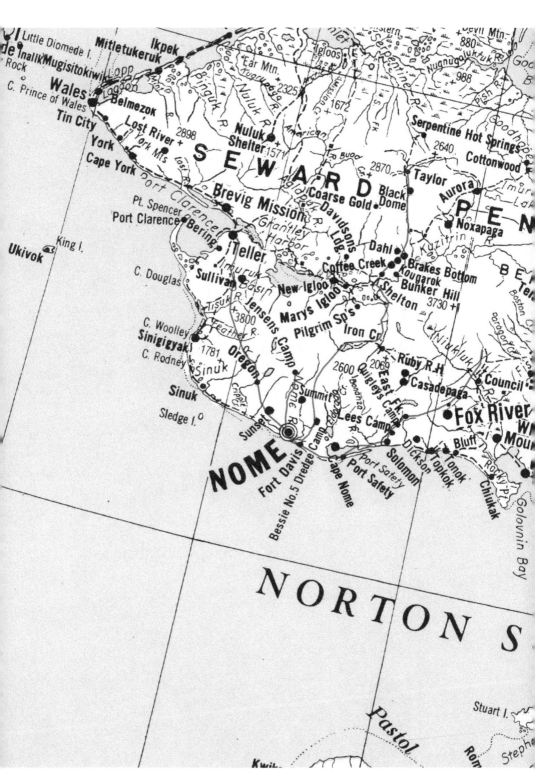

Introduction

♦ ♦ ♦

"Where in the hell is St. Lawrence Island?" Tod asked, laughing, when I telephoned him about a telegram from the Bureau of Indian Affairs (BIA) that had been delivered to my apartment in Boulder, Colorado.

"Pick me up after your class," I replied, "We'll go to the library to see if we can find it."

The BIA telegram read: "Wire collect if you

▲ *Charles "Tod" Ray and I met on a blind date, but we were not one another's date. Tod was studying at the University of Colorado. I was teaching there.*
◄ *Overleaf spread: We soon "found" St. Lawrence Island in the Bering Sea.*

will accept a two-teacher appointment to the elementary school at Savoonga, St. Lawrence Island, Alaska. If offer is accepted, additional information will be sent by mail."

It was July 1951. Charles "Tod" Ray and I, Doris Derby, the two of us just 23, were engaged to be married in August, having met on a double date two years before at the University of Colorado. Tod's roommate had been my date, while Tod, I observed, was with a cute young "chick." Later, Tod and I came to enjoy one another's company, meeting occasionally for coffee or a beer, and our friendship blossomed into a romantic relationship.

We had come of age just as World War II was winding down. The fighting was nearing an end in the spring of 1945. However, Congress had not formally recognized an end to the war until spring 1946 when Tod graduated from high school in Gunnison, Colorado. He had been raised by his mother, a widow whose husband had died when Tod was 5. Because young men still were subject to the draft, Tod chose to enlist in the Army.

Meanwhile, as an active teenager growing up in a comfortable middle-class home in Detroit, I contributed to the war effort by collecting scrap metals for manufacture of armaments and saving cooking fats for making explosives. The city had boomed during the early 1940s with the production of tanks, trucks, and airplanes.

After college in Detroit and graduate studies at Clark University in Worcester, Massachusetts, where I earned an M.A. in history, I was offered a position at the University of Colorado teaching western civilization while continuing my doctoral studies in Slavic history.

Tod served with the U.S. occupation force in post-war Japan, then joined millions of other veterans who were enrolling in American universities under the Servicemen's Readjustment Act, known fondly as the "G.I. Bill of Rights." Enacted by Congress in 1944, the program provided free tuition and expenses.

Tod finished his undergraduate studies with a B.A. in English just in time for our wedding. Coincidentally, he had taken a course in western civ, though he was not in my class. This was just as well, I think.

On a whim, we had applied for BIA teaching jobs after discovering we shared concerns about the state of Indian education.

In the Southwest U.S., there was growing public awareness that the principal institutions for educating thousands of young Native Americans were boarding schools, established and/or supported by the BIA and other governmental agencies. These young students were forced to live far from home, forbidden to use their own names, speak their languages, wear traditional clothing, and practice their religion. They were frequent targets of verbal and physical abuse.

We digested general information from the BIA but heard nothing specific about potential employment. Tod had been offered a position teaching English in a Denver suburb beginning in the autumn and was close to signing a contract when the telegram arrived.

At the library, we found a Rand McNally map of the vast Alaska Territory, which was larger than Texas, California, and Montana combined. Beginning at the southeast corner near Ketchikan, we slowly traced the coastline, moving west and then north, until we came upon St. Lawrence Island. Situated in the northern Bering Sea about 150 miles south of the Bering Strait and much closer to Siberia

(36 miles from the Chukchi Peninsula) than to Nome on the Seward Peninsula (164 miles away). The island was about 90 miles long and 8 to 22 miles wide.

A brief *Encyclopedia Americana* entry described a treeless tundra with two small Yupik villages—Savoonga (1950 population 249), Gambell (population 309)—and a herd of 10,000 reindeer. The island's average low temperature in January was about 5° Fahrenheit and the average high in July about 50° F. St. Lawrence received more than five feet of snow annually. Later, we learned first-hand of the fierce winds that battered the island in winter.

After much discussion, we concluded we had been offered an opportunity for a unique experience that we should take advantage of—for at least one year—before moving on with our professional lives and family responsibilities. Accordingly, we sent a telegram to the BIA accepting the positions.

I saw little of Tod the next few weeks as he finished his coursework. We talked by phone. I began making the travel arrangements with the BIA, ordering supplies, and organizing the shipment of our few belongings to Savoonga.

Because the small co-op store in Savoonga stocked few groceries, we would have to place a large order for food to last the entire school year. I was in a quandary: what to order? I had never prepared meals for two people for a week, let alone for a year.

Time was running short. Our order had to be put aboard a government freighter, the *North Star,* which was leaving Seattle on its second and last Alaska trip of the year on August 1, in about two weeks' time.

Fortunately, the BIA was helpful as we planned the 3,000-mile move to remote St. Lawrence Island. Especially welcome was a detailed list of recommended groceries and dry goods that could be ordered from a Seattle wholesaler and delivered directly to the *North Star.* Neither of us had sufficient funds to purchase a year's worth of food, so the BIA offered to pay for the order and deduct funds from our salaries to reimburse the government.

Between us, we would earn approximately $8,000[1] plus a 25% cost-of-living allowance for the school year. We would rent the teachers' quarters attached to the school for $12 a month.

Finally came the last week of August. Tod's commencement at the University of Colorado took place on Saturday, August 25. The next day, our families and a few friends gathered in Denver for a small wedding at an Episcopal church, followed by a reception and dinner that evening.

On Monday, we rented two cars and drove into the nearby Rocky Mountains for a day of sight-seeing with our respective families, whom we might not see

---

1. Adjusting for inflation, the equivalent value in 2023 was more than $90,000.

▲ *Tod and I said good-bye to our mothers after our wedding.*

for some time. Tod and his mother spent a wonderful day together. Sadly, it was the last time he saw her. She died a year and a half later at a time when winter weather prevented Tod from flying off St. Lawrence Island.

Bright and early on Tuesday, August 28, we boarded a Union Pacific train bound for the Pacific Northwest. I wore my going-away outfit: a suit, gabardine coat, and a close-fitting green velour hat trimmed with a long pheasant feather—quite chic, I thought.

My mother, understandably upset that her only child was going to the "far ends of the earth," as she put it, informed me that I could not go to my new home without a house plant. So, she presented me with one. Off I went with Tod, carrying in my lap an African violet we named Virgil.

Little did we know this journey north would mark a major turning point in our lives.

Little did we know this journey north would mark a major turning point in our lives.

▲ *Indian men fished for salmon with long-handled dip-nets from high scaffolds overlooking the Columbia River between Washington and Oregon.*

1

On Our Way

■

There are no roads.
Savoonga has no airstrip.
Winter air service to Gambell is
limited until Troutman Lake freezes
hard and airplanes can
land on the ice.

❖ ❖ ❖

SEATTLE
Thursday, August 30, 1951

Dear Mother and Glad,

We arrived in Seattle last night after an uneventful 36 hours on the train. Frankly, most of the trip was boring, especially the hours and hours passing through southern Wyoming. We saw little but sagebrush in all directions and an occasional herd of antelope in the distance.

Thankfully, our seats had leg rests, so we were fairly comfortable. Tod says I spent most of the night sprawled on his seat as well as on my own. I cannot dispute his claim.

The scenery certainly improved when the train reached the Columbia River. We followed this big river for about 200 miles to Portland, Oregon. For thousands of years, Indian tribes have used the waterway for travel, trade, and fishing. Even for the Lewis and Clark Expedition, the Columbia was a water route to the explorers' destination, the Pacific Ocean.

We passed several Indian villages where the men fished with long-handled dip-nets from high scaffolds overlooking the river. It looked dangerous!

The last 80 miles took us through the 4,000-foot-deep Columbia River Gorge, a breath-taking stretch of river that forms a boundary between the states of Oregon and Washington as it flows through the Cascade Mountains.

In Portland, we transferred onto a Northern Pacific passenger train. Five hours later, we marveled at the elegance of the King Street Station on our arrival in Seattle and then checked into the Stewart Hotel near the Pike Place Market.

The next morning the BIA "processed" us as federal employees and gave us a stack of documents to sign. Later, we opened a charge account at Sears, Roebuck & Co., which offers special discounts to Alaska teachers. I bought four pairs of knee socks and some red underwear.

When we got back to the hotel, Tod wanted to go down to the bar and order a beer so that he could watch television for the first time. We watched *Howdy Doody*. Tod was not impressed.

Much Love, Doris

❖ ❖ ❖

JUNEAU
Monday, September 3, 1951

Dear Mother,

On Sunday morning, we flew on a Pan Am DC-6 to Juneau, arriving here about 2 p.m. It was a pleasant flight. We were served two excellent meals as we flew in and out of the thick clouds, thrilled to see the snow-topped peaks and massive glaciers far below.

Juneau, the territorial capital, is nestled at the foot of two steep mountains along Gastineau Channel. Population: about 8,000. This quaint little town has a couple of hotels, a few restaurants, a gold mine, and lots of salmon. It is a terribly expensive place to live. Juneau prices are about twice those of the States.

Today, we had a talk with an education specialist from the Alaska Native Service (ANS), an agency of the U.S. Bureau of Indian Affairs (BIA), who told us some of what to expect in Savoonga and answered our many questions. Apparently, we will have considerably more school supplies than we expected.

You will be interested to know the school has subscriptions to a variety of magazines including *Life, National Geographic, Time, Good Housekeeping, Popular Mechanics,* and *Popular Science.* This will help with teaching and keep us posted on news from "Outside," the term Alaskans use referring to any place beyond the boundaries of the Territory.

That's all for now. I'm beginning to imagine the school year ahead. I can see we will be busy.

Love, Doris

❖ ❖ ❖

NOME

Dear Mother,

What a week!

After meetings in Juneau, we flew in a Pacific Northern Airlines DC-3 to Anchorage, Alaska's largest city. Population: about 11,000. The city is growing fast. After World War II, millions of dollars were spent here on a buildup of troops and military facilities for defense, including expansion of Fort Richardson and Elmendorf Air Force Base. The high prices in Alaska continue to amaze us. I don't see how people here survive.

On Thursday, we flew in an Alaska Airlines DC-3 to Nome, a former gold-rush town on the Bering Sea. It is about what you would expect—13 bars for a population of around 2,000. An Air Force squadron at the Nome Airport broadcasts excellent music and news programs from the Armed Forces Radio System. I hope we will be able to pick up AFRS on St. Lawrence Island.

We talked by short-wave radio with Tim Gologergen, the teachers' aide in Savoonga. Tim, an Eskimo[2], is well-known and respected among the ANS staff in Nome. He has been teaching the middle grades, so I guess I'll take the lower grades. We are told the children are extremely shy, and the little ones often cry when frightened. I will do my best not to frighten them.

I'll teach the little ones for two hours in the morning and another two hours in the afternoon. An hour will be devoted to teaching the older girls a little sewing, knitting, and simple cooking. Tod will teach a shop class for the older boys. On Mondays and Wednesdays, I will have a music class for the older children. We'll have a lot of fun. I'm told the children are not shy about singing.

The Eskimo villagers on the island speak Yupik and are related more to the Siberian natives than to the mainland Eskimos who speak Inupiaq. Because the two languages are so different, English is the only common language used by the Eskimos (and by all Alaska natives) to communicate with one another.

Our main mission will be to teach English. In our orientation, we learned that we will not teach the standard academic courses for elementary students. Instead, we are to concentrate on language skills, health care, home economics, and other practical subjects intended to improve the peoples' lives.

In addition to teaching, Tod also will serve as the village's unofficial doctor, welfare agent, agent of law and order, conservation officer, and advisor to both the Village Council and the store, which operates with a loan from the federal government.

---

2. A term widely used in 1951 and for decades afterward, "Eskimo" is a word invented by outsiders as a catch-all name for the indigenous Inupiaq and Yupik people.

During our layover in Nome, the ANS nurse instructed us on how to deal with serious illnesses. In an emergency, because Savoonga has neither a doctor nor a nurse, we are expected to consult with an ANS doctor in Kotzebue by short-wave radio. The doctor takes such calls from the villages at 6 p.m. every day. We report the patient's temperature, symptoms, and other observations. The doctor then recommends treatment.

For less serious illnesses, we are on our own. The school has a clinic with all kinds of medicines, including penicillin, to treat infections; sulfathiazole powder, a short-acting antibiotic; cathartics, a laxative; opiates, for pain relief; and phenobarbital, to treat seizures, among other symptoms.

The nurse showed us how to give hypodermic injections. She also explained what to do if there are complications in a childbirth. The village has its own midwives, but in case of trouble we may be asked for help. Thankfully, a nurse will be posted to Savoonga in January.

If you don't see regular mail from us, be patient. Our letters may reach you in batches. This time of year, we will receive mail twice a month, so that's when our mail goes out, too. Received a letter from you yesterday. We intercepted it at the Nome Post Office before it was sent to Savoonga.

This morning we walked down to the camp of King Island Eskimos on the outskirts of Nome and watched the ivory-carvers at work. We hear there is much ivory-carving on St. Lawrence, too, so you may expect that we will send our Christmas gifts from there. Hint, hint.

Love, Doris

P.S. from Tod: You might be interested to know that in Anchorage we picked up a begonia, which we named Billy, to keep company with the African Violet (Virgil) you gave us. Billy and Virgil are both surviving the long travel days.

❖ ❖ ❖

This time of year, we will receive mail twice a month, so that's when our mail goes out, too. Received a letter from you yesterday.

GAMBELL

Dear Mother,

We are almost there! On Sunday, we hitched a ride from Nome to Gambell in an Army PBY "flying boat" that landed on Troutman Lake next to the village. Gambell is the only other village on the island. There are no roads here. Savoonga has no airstrip. Winter air service to Gambell is limited until Troutman Lake freezes hard and airplanes can land on the ice.

We arrived here about 2:30 p.m. Too late to go on to Savoonga. So, we spent the night with the teachers at the Gambell school. They have two small children who were noisy and, I must say, spoiled. Consequently, we didn't get much rest, as we were sleeping on a hide-a-bed in the living room.

We thought we would depart Monday morning. But we awoke to high winds and rough seas—a blustery Northwester. No travel that day. We have been stuck here ever since.

Thankfully, the wind had died down this morning. We contacted Savoonga by short-wave radio to check the weather there. Conditions were good, so we expect to leave in about an hour. I must get this letter in the mail.

Did I mention getting to Savoonga requires a five- or six-hour run along the Bering Sea coast in an open *umiak*, a skinboat made by stretching walrus skins across a frame made from whale bones or driftwood?

Don't worry, it's safe. I'll tell you all about it in my next letter.

Love, Doris

2

Warm Welcome

*I was surprised and
pleased. It seemed as if every
man, woman, and child in Savoonga
had come down to greet us,
waving and smiling.*

❖ ❖ ❖

SAVOONGA
Tuesday, September 18, 1951

Dear Mother,

I have so much to tell you! In less than two weeks, our lives have become so vastly different from anything we have ever experienced or even imagined.

▲ *The village was established as a permanent settlement in the 1930s near the site of a reindeer herders' camp.*

After the delay in Gambell, the winds finally died down and the seas calmed. About noon, we set out for Savoonga in an open walrus skinboat. It looked to be about twice the length and width of a standard canoe. A weather forecaster might have described the day as "fair" because of the sunshine, but let me tell you, it was COLD!

I must confess, we were poorly dressed for the damp, cold, breezy air and the occasional splash of seawater as the skinboat made its way through rolling waves. We had on the same summer clothes we wore on the train in August. Tod: suede jacket, khaki pants, loafers, and thin socks. Me: slacks, loafers,

▲ *Missionary Alice Green, left, Tod, and I were the only white people in a village of about 250 Yupik Eskimos.*

light-weight socks, my fashionable gabardine coat, and the fancy hat with the long pheasant feather. My houseplants were still in a box on my lap. We must have been a strange sight, two innocents huddled among the three grizzled, weather-hardened crewmen who wore waterproof parkas.

We could see low volcanic hills in the distance as we cut across the mouth of a wide bay, covering the 40 miles to Savoonga in a little more than five hours—good time, we were told. Along the way, we saw several large *ookgruk* seals and many sea birds but little else in the vast, empty Bering Sea.

As we neared land, the village came into view—two dozen or so modest frame dwellings with the school and a single church standing out. Wooden sidewalks provided dry pathways above the marshy tundra.

The first thing we heard were dogs barking with excitement. It seems we were the main event of the day.

Stiff, sore, and bone weary, we climbed unsteadily out of the skinboat onto the gravelly shore where we were welcomed by the Presbyterian missionary. Until our arrival, she had been the only non-native in the village.

"Welcome to Savoonga. I'm Alice Green."

"Hello. I'm Doris Derby," I replied.

"Oh, I thought the Rays were coming today—the new teachers." Alice said, looking confused.

"Oh, yes, we ARE the new teachers. I'm Doris RAY." This was the first time I'd identified myself with my new surname.

Mother, even though I was nervous, I was also surprised and pleased. It seemed as if every man, woman, and child in Savoonga had come down to greet us, waving and smiling. Tod and I were flush with excitement. We shook hands with about 50 villagers. Most were friendly but quiet. Nearly everyone wore boots and were clad in what we learned were "snowshirts," heavy-cotton garments pulled over their parkas, or worn alone in mild weather. The men's pullovers were plain and unadorned, mostly white and tan. The women's snowshirts were brightly colored, and patterns decorated the hemlines.

Before long, Alice Green hustled us off for a hot meal in the manse attached to the church. Alice, a spinster, has represented the Presbyterian Church in Savoonga since 1945.

Although she has said nothing, Alice, I suspect, is lonesome here with no family and few friends. Since our arrival, she has visited at least once a day and has invited us to her place several times for meals.

On our second night here, Alice hosted a reception in our honor at the church. Again, nearly all the villagers turned out. Tod and I felt honored, but also nervous. The choir sang a traditional Savoonga song of welcome (in Yupik, of course), and Alice made a speech. We were lucky to be teaching in Savoonga, she

▲ *The village was connected by a network of boardwalks.*

said. Then Tod stood up. School would start soon, he said, and we were looking forward to getting to know the children and others.

Tod revealed that we are newlyweds. But he said nothing about the ink still being wet on his diploma. We heard the women whispering to Alice as they prepared to serve the coffee and cookies.

"So young!" . . . "Very young."

After the speeches, Alice urged everyone to mingle. No one moved. Finally, Tod and I rose and walked around rather awkwardly, smiling nervously and trying to be cordial. It seemed as if about 500 eyes followed us. It must be true what we had heard: people here are reticent in dealing with outsiders.

After more pleading from Alice, a few brave souls got up and headed for the refreshment table. By the time the shindig ended, a few villagers had approached us to shake hands before bolting for the door. Alice said not to worry. The custom, she said, is for everyone to come individually to the teachers' quarters to welcome us, so we expect a parade of visitors in the next few days.

Despite their reticent demeanor, the villagers already have made us feel welcome, and we are eager to teach their children and get to know everyone.

More later.

Love, Doris

▲ *The Bureau of Indian Affairs was responsible for teaching Alaska natives in their villages. These six cuties were in my first class.*

Indian Education

Perspective: Native education in rural Alaska was changing

SLOWLY but steadily, education in native villages was undergoing major changes when we arrived in Alaska.

During the early decades after the purchase of Alaska from Russian in 1867, native education had been carried out mostly by missionaries in remote areas while segregated schools were established in Sitka and Juneau.

In 1905, Congress passed the Nelson Act giving the federal Bureau of Indian Affairs (BIA) responsibility for educating Alaska natives in their villages. The territorial government, meanwhile, would educate non-natives and "children of mixed blood who lead a civilized life" in the cities.

For the next several decades, BIA programs encouraged the native people to accept western values, beliefs, language, and customs while helping them to develop self-reliance and citizenship.

This federal policy was predicated on the idea that acculturation would occur mostly in rural areas where the natives would continue to live.

To this end, the BIA's Alaska Native Service (ANS) undertook ambitious social programs to improve the condition of the native people. Hospitals were built, medical

supplies were sent to village teachers, social welfare programs were initiated, and funds for the relief of destitution were appropriated. Economic assistance was provided through the encouragement of native industries such as ivory-carving and the establishment of native cooperative stores.

The village school was the focal point for the federal programs. BIA teachers came to be considered social workers whose duties might also include those of physicians, nurses, postmasters, business managers, community builders, and village advisors.

The BIA's education plan was expanded beyond the teaching of English. The new curriculum included instruction in sanitation and personal hygiene. Vocational education included instruction in manual arts such as carpentry and domestic science including cooking, sewing, and other household skills.

World War II resulted in population shifts and increasing job opportunities throughout the Territory. As a result, the BIA adopted new policies to move natives toward a "complete assimilation into the culture and economy of Alaska" and prepare them to live anywhere in Alaska, not just in their isolated villages.

However, by the time we arrived, the post-war assimilation programs had not yet "seeped down" to the villages. Consequently, in the autumn of 1951, our orientation and assignments continued to reflect the traditional role of the village school as "community center."

▲ *The BIA school, to which our quarters were attached, also served as a part-time clinic and community center on a bluff overlooking the sea.*

3

First Days

◾

*Our food order for a year is
on the* North Star, *which has been
delayed for about a month.
We're wondering, what will
we to eat until then?*

❖ ❖ ❖

Sunday, September 16, 1951

Dear Mom and Ashfords,

As you can imagine, everything here is new, different, and—at times—difficult. Today I've been learning the tricks of operating the light plant for our quarters, which are attached to the school.

We're also acquainting ourselves with the procedures for transmitting and receiving messages by short-wave radio. I am the telegram agent for Savoonga as the school has the village's only short-wave station. There is little privacy for radio calls and telegrams, however, since most households have a radio receiver.

I should add that in an emergency, you can get in touch with us quickly by sending a telegram. Address it to Savoonga, Alaska, "via Nome," where it will be relayed to us on a scheduled radio transmission from the Alaska Communications System (ACS).

My medical responsibilities already have me pulling my hair out. Part of my assignment is to operate a medical clinic. I know little about prescribing and administering medicine.

Today, a mother came to the clinic with a little boy who had a swollen gland in his neck that was causing him all sorts of grief. The last time he was x-rayed, the boy's left lung was found to be full of tuberculosis. I did not know if there was a connection between the TB and his swollen gland, but I prescribed hot packs for his neck and gave him some APC tablets (containing aspirin, phenacetin, and caffeine) to counter the swelling and deaden the pain.

I may have told you earlier that the ANS nurse in Nome had given us hurried directions for delivering babies in case we are called on to assist. Several deaths have occurred here because of the placenta becoming lodged in the birth canal. The midwives have been known to step on the stomachs of women in labor to hasten the birth. We were advised to discourage such practices, but not to get involved in every obstetric case that comes along. The mission of the ANS, we were informed, is to educate the native people on subjects mainly related to health and hygiene, and to avoid creating undue dependence on non-natives. This philosophy impressed me immensely. I still can't picture myself delivering a baby.

It appears we will be able to start school the day after tomorrow. We have spent the past couple of days getting ready while also working to make our quarters more livable. With help from our teacher-aide, Tim Gologergen, we applied a kalsomine wash to the living-room walls, cleaned the furniture and dressers, and took stock of what we have in the way of food and school supplies. Things will probably be rocky for the first week or so. *C'est la guerre!*

I don't know when this mail will go out. Likely you will receive several letters in a bunch when the villagers begin sledding mail out to Gambell. Dogsled transportation should resume the last of this month, for even now the sea is becoming mighty rough. Few days remain during which the skinboats will be able to make safe trips between Gambell and Savoonga.

Love as always, Tod

❖ ❖ ❖

Tuesday, September 18, 1951

Dear Mother,

I'm picking up where I left off in my last letter.

While in Juneau, we discovered our food order is on the *North Star*, which has been delayed for about a month. We're wondering, what will we eat until then? The food in the store is terribly expensive and the choices are limited. Alice Green has been lending us essential food from her own limited pantry.

At any rate, do not worry! Tod and I are nowhere near starving. I promise I will never again take for granted a fully stocked grocery store.

The worst aspect of our life here so far has been the poor condition of our living quarters. However, we have been working on this, and our new home is beginning to look livable. Our quarters come with a kerosene refrigerator, an oil range, a typewriter, and a vacuum. An oil stove in the living room, along with the kitchen stove, is our sole source of heat. The bedrooms can be quite chilly! Electricity for the building comes from two generators housed in the utility room at the back of the school.

Next summer, we will wash off the kalsomine and give the house a proper painting. The government will provide the paint and even pay for some labor.

Our chemical toilet is a bugbear, but so far Tod has emptied it without difficulty. This unpleasant chore must be done about once a week.

Teaching in Savoonga is considerably different than teaching in the States. The school has 90 students. There are 29 in my class and the other two classes are about the same size. The children are exceedingly shy, so there are few discipline problems. But our difficulty is persuading the kids to tell us where they are in their schoolbooks. They haven't been willing to speak up in the classroom. But I think I am making progress.

Because the little ones do not read, I am introducing them to the alphabet and simple numbers. I am playing some children's learning songs, too, such as *Farmer in the Dell*. The challenge is more getting the kids acquainted with being together and learning English than teaching them standard academic subjects.

The school has a small, new organ that I claimed for my classroom. Every day for about 30 minutes we sing songs such as *London Bridge is Falling Down* and play games. Some of the images—bridges, farms, cows, the dell, and so forth—are alien to the children. But they seem eager to learn new things, and we are making do with the teaching materials we have.

Mae Kingeekuk, a short, round woman in her forties, is making me a pair of *mukluks* (boots) from reindeer hide with soles of tough sealskin. She plans to trim the tops with the fur of unborn seals. These boots will keep my feet warm and dry on all occasions.

Mae is a good-natured woman with an infectious laugh. We are becoming good friends. I was a little taken aback to learn Mae will trim the *mukluks* with the fur of unborn seals. Apparently, this fur is extraordinary in its softness. When I expressed surprise at the source of the fur, Mae explained that in their culture NOTHING that can be used goes to waste.

St. Lawrence Island is the best place in Alaska to find ivory because of the large numbers of walruses. The villagers have achieved a high level of a unique art in their carving of the ivory. Theodore Kingeekuk, Mae's husband, is thought to be one of most skilled and artistic carvers on the island.

Theodore and Mae Kingeekuk seem typical of married couples here. Mr. Kingeekuk and his sons hunt for walruses, seals, and the occasional whale to feed the family. Mae, an excellent seamstress, preserves the meat, tans the skins, and does the usual household chores. She and her daughters also put away the bedding each morning because her family, like most others, sleeps side-by-side on the floor.

By the way, you'd better get used to our letters arriving on an irregular basis. During the winter, Alaska Airlines flies into Gambell every two weeks. Joseph Noongwook, our mail carrier, takes mail to Gambell by dogsled and returns with mail for Savoonga. In the summer, mail between the villages is carried by skinboat. From Gambell, outgoing mail moves to Nome, and new mail is brought back on the occasional Army plane. None of the planes comes to Savoonga. It is not uncommon for poor weather to delay the mail for long periods.

I don't know when this letter will go out, but you will probably get several in a bunch when the villagers begin sledding the mail.

Well, it's time for bed. Will write again soon.

Love, Ted, and Doris

Each sled was pulled by eight to twelve dog

▲ A musher and his dog team returned home at dusk with a piece of lumber scavenged from the sea.

P.S. I wish you could see the view of the Bering Sea we have from our living-room windows. The school building with our quarters attached sits near a rocky cliff on a high cape that is constantly assaulted by powerful winds and waves. It is every bit what you might imagine a wild ocean to be. The school faces north, but we are somewhat protected as our quarters are attached on the south side of the school building. Our living room faces west.

4

Settling in

■

The textbook describes
children visiting a
circus and riding a bus.
My little ones have no idea
what a circus is and have
never seen a bus.

❖ ❖ ❖

Thursday, September 27, 1951

Dear Mother,

We are busy! Our days are filled with teaching and fulfilling various other responsibilities assigned to us.

Tod has been working long hours due to a summer flu epidemic spreading through the village. He visits patients after school and then again after his nightly radio consultation with the government doctor in Kotzebue. The doctor's prescriptions are relatively simple: bed rest and aspirin. And if the patient's temperature rises above 101°, administer a shot of penicillin.

Meanwhile, villagers continue to come to the clinic steadily with all sorts of other ailments. I suspect some have cases of hypochondria.

Alice Green has been ill. I stopped in to check on her and make tea several times a day last week. She is better now—at least well enough to come to our place for dinner.

My first attempt to bake bread was a disappointment. I may not have kneaded the dough enough. I might try again on Saturday. Tod said he would help me knead, as he knows all about making bread from watching his mother. That I seriously doubt!

My living room looks much better now. Tod kalsomined the wall a pale green, and we have a new green carpet. We expect a new green frieze sofa-bed to arrive on the *North Star*, but for now we are using a blue davenport from the

▲ *Julia Alowa, Nellie Seppilu, and Jenny Alowa pose for a photo.*

empty nurse's quarters in the old schoolhouse. We also have a maple drop-leaf table between the windows. A brass lamp looks attractive with its flowered shade. I hung plastic drapes that I brought with me. They give the place a homey look.

I am fixing a bowl of artificial flowers to sit on top of one of the bookcases. We also have two comfortable armchairs and a hideous little rocker that I plan to recover as soon as I can order some material from Sears in Seattle.

Last night, Alice and I ordered fabric from Sears to use for a snowshirt over a parka that Mae Kingeekuk will make for me from an Army blanket I found here. Usually, the women's parkas are made from a heavy blanket lined with flannelette. They come down to just below the knees and often are trimmed around the bottom with white fur, sometimes from unborn dogs. The St. Lawrence Island women use black rabbit fur around the hood for trim. Over the parka the women wear a cotton snowshirt of brightly printed cotton that, like a dress, can be changed on occasion.

The new parka will keep me warm on almost any occasion, except when riding in a dogsled. For dogsled travel, Alice says she will lend me her heavy reindeer parka.

▲ *My little ones, the cutest kids I've ever seen, remained still long enough to pose for a class photograph on the school steps.*

In the past, parkas were made from reindeer hides. Reindeer are scarce now, however, as the island no longer has a large reindeer herd. Many of the men have army-surplus parkas lined with alpaca fiber that is soft, warm, and strong. Tod has ordered one from the store in Nome.

The government has provided us two pairs of leather ski pants lined with sheepskin. We both want to get a pair of fur socks made to wear inside our *mukluks*. They are shaped something like a regular sock but function more like a high-sided bedroom slipper. They can be slipped on and off easily and worn like wool loafer-socks with leather soles. They will be grand for use as bedroom slippers around the house, too.

I don't know if we are making progress at school. The children are so shy! They won't talk and merely stare at me when I speak to them. I have been drawing onto cards pictures of familiar Alaskan things such as boots and parkas, with the English word written underneath. So far, there has been little response. Everyone says the children will come out of their shells after they get to know me better. I certainly hope so. I am frustrated, and my patience is wearing thin. Tod has been discouraged with his older students, too. They are at a complete loss when it comes to any oral situation. The adults are always polite and willing to help.

I have a sewing class this afternoon. We are making pin-cushions. I must confess, I feel foolish teaching this class. I can't teach these older girls any more than they already know. Most of the girls make fur parkas and boots so, the truth is, they know more about sewing than I do.

I have an idea. I may have my sewing class dress one of the dolls in a native costume and then send the doll to the children at your school. In return, perhaps your children would send my little ones some old toys like blocks, tiny cars, and so forth. My beginners don't have toys, and they need to be able to play and build things.

Well, I must stop and get lunch. I don't know when this letter will get off the island. I can mail it quickly if I hear a skinboat is leaving for Gambell on short notice.

Love, Doris and Tod

❖ ❖ ❖

Tuesday, October 16, 1951

Dear Eunice,

We still await the arrival of the government ship, the *North Star,* with our year's supply of groceries and the assortment of boxes sent from Denver and Detroit with our bedding, towels, and other household items.

We will be able to buy reindeer meat when the *North Star* arrives. Part of the reindeer herd was butchered on Nunivak Island off the southwest Alaska coast, and the *North Star* is bringing some of the carcasses for sale on St. Lawrence. The meat tastes much like beef, only more tender, so we look forward eagerly to having a big reindeer feast. If the weather stays cold enough, I think we will buy a half. We should be able to keep it frozen in a locker under the school.

Our water supply is a major problem. We have ordered a pump to bring water during the summer from the creek, which is about 300 yards from the school, to a large storage tank in our utility room at the rear of the building. Meanwhile, Tod and some of the older boys are carrying water in pails.

▲ *Sled dogs were tethered near a stream that was our source of water during the summer months. We boiled the water before drinking it.*

▲ During the cold-weather months, we hired villagers to cut large blocks
of ice from a nearby lake and bring them to the school on sleds.

▲ The blocks were stacked; then Tod moved ice to a storage tank, as needed, to melt for
household and school use. Drinking water was boiled.

Last weekend, Tod splurged by carrying in two large containers full of water so we could take real baths in the bathtub. We heated the water on the stove. It was the most enjoyable evening I've spent since leaving Seattle. You would never think that a plain, ordinary bath could be such a treat. We've almost decided to do this once a week, provided our water supplier (Tod) holds out and the water pipes under the bathtub don't freeze.

During the winter, we have a special fund to pay for having ice cut and melted. The villagers cut large blocks from a nearby lake and bring it to the school by dogsled. We store it on a rack behind our shed. It is then brought into the storage tank, as needed, to melt. I keep a large pot of boiled water on our kitchen counter for drinking and cooking.

I have started a program in my class to encourage and reward good hygiene. Each morning, I inspect everyone's nails, face, hands, ears, and neck, and then check to see if the children's hair is combed. I am making a wall chart to record the results. The children who are clean get a piece of candy.

This program has shown positive results! The six- and seven-year-olds are coming to school looking polished and anticipating their rewards.

These are the cutest children I have ever seen. They are never rude, nor are they showoffs, although my little ones are becoming more confident and are beginning to slap each other playfully when my back is turned. I consider this to be a sign of progress.

Well, Tod just rang the last bell, so I must get to work. Will write again soon.
Love, Doris

❖ ❖ ❖

Dear Eunice, Pappy, and Boys,

I'll add this note to Doris's letter. Despite the inconvenience of living in an isolated village, there are few if any out-of-pocket expenses. I never have lived in a place where I could walk around for a month with 50 cents in my pocket and never have a need to spend it. No parking meters, no Salvation Army boxes, no newsstands, no drug stores, just plain nothing requiring cash.

The government, while hell on taxpayers, is rather considerate of its employees. We are going to buy our reindeer, butchered on Nunivak Island, for 35 cents a pound—a bargain! It will come in on the *North Star*. Already we are considering sticking it out here for a second year. Our decision will depend on how well we survive the weather and how weary we become in mid-winter of darkness from mid-afternoon until about 10 the next morning.

My main headache, other than getting rather poor results at school, is my role as an unlicensed doctor. I am in frequent radio contact with an ANS doctor, but 90% of this job is left to my imagination. Last week, I was instructed to give shots of penicillin to a little baby about one year old. Naturally, my only experience with shots had been as a recipient, so I was rather at a loss, except I knew generally that you jabbed them and squirted in the goop.

I was squeamish about poking a man-sized needle into the rump of a tiny child, but orders are orders. Before I touched him with the needle, he already was screaming and making a fuss. To make matters worse, the entire family was standing around watching my performance and—I imagined—judging it. To make an embarrassing story short, I never did inoculate the baby, though I pricked him with the needle a few times. Finally, I let his uncle do it. He had given shots before and knew the kid well.

Since then, I have been more successful. It isn't hard once you get the fact that you must stick them hard and not be chicken-hearted.

Teaching here has been a let-down. Maybe I am too fresh out of a college classroom, but all my efforts are hampered by the fact that the only English these kids speak is in the school during school hours. They speak Yupik at home. So, trying to teach them history, story problems in math, science, and other subjects comes off like the proverbial water off a duck's back. The natural strategy, then, is to teach them words they NEED to know and names of some of the objects THEY HAVE SEEN BEFORE. Maybe I will become inspired and feel at some future date that I am making progress—I surely hope so.

The events of the community, while mostly routine, nevertheless provide Doris and me with lots to talk about. I am beginning to feel a little guilty for allowing tidbits of gossip about the affairs of the community to provide us with

▲ *The kids were shy, well-behaved, and mostly eager to learn.*

leisure enjoyment, but we cannot help it. I suppose were Savoonga villagers to visit our homes in the States, they would find aspects of life there to be amusing as well.

On a recent evening, there was a meeting of the Village Council, of which I am an honorary member. Government employees are admonished to keep their hands out of the affairs of the native community and to merely advise, if necessary. The seven-member council discussed community problems, one of them being a few of the older boys are getting high from sniffing fumes of gasoline they stole from one of the villagers. No alcohol is allowed. Savoonga and Gambell are dry villages, by edict of the village councils.

The council then turned to the business of electing a new member to replace the council president, who died recently. (Untimely deaths are common here, for there is much disease and many accidents. About one of every three villagers has tuberculosis.) The council members asked me if I thought having an election was a good idea, and, of course, I stated that electing a councilman to take the place of the one who had died was a fine idea. After some haggling, the council decided to vote by secret ballot after three men were nominated. They asked me to vote, but naturally I declined.

After a preliminary vote to eliminate one candidate, the ballot was narrowed to two men. Here they hit a snag. Each of the two candidates received three votes. With the council president gone, and no one taking his place, there was no one to break the tie. The council haggled in Yupik for some time and decided that I should break the tie. This was the council's problem, I did not know the candidates, and I did not want to take sides. So, I explained again that I was not qualified to vote. Someone translated my comment into Yupik, and they kicked it around for a while.

Finally, a man who spoke broken English said, "Oh, that okay, we vote for Alaska legislature all time and we not know nobody—we just guess vote." I explained parliamentary procedure and got them debating the merits of each candidate. Finally, after the fourth vote, the tie was broken.

This has become a lengthy tale. However, I wanted to make my point that the community keeps us engaged. Contrary to expectations, I haven't had time to be lonely yet, since I am surrounded by people.

Well, it is time for my evening radio broadcast, so I'll stop for now. Write often, even though we only get mail every month or so.

Love as always, Tod

❖ ❖ ❖

Sunday, October 28, 1951

Dear Mother,

The *North Star* STILL has not arrived!

The ship was to have been here last Sunday, but the weather turned stormy, and it was held up for four days. It finally got back to Gambell on Friday, unloaded freight there on Saturday, and was to be in Savoonga this morning. But as luck would have it, the good weather we have had for the past couple of days disappeared this morning, replaced by a howling wind gusting to about 60 miles an hour.

So, the ship is still at Gambell and will remain there until the weather clears. No telling how long that will be.

We are terribly disappointed. We had hoped to get our mail and food supplies and anticipated having a huge meal tonight. We are starving for variety.

The meat supply in the school lunch pantry consists of canned sausages. Alice Green's meager food supply is surprisingly limited, too. I don't see how she can get by for a year on such a small selection of food, especially as she must eat the same thing at breakfast, lunch, and dinner to keep food from spoiling. The only milk we have, other than evaporated, is dried powdered milk, so we have been practically living on cocoa. When our own powdered milk comes, I will make it to drink, as we have ordered quite a bit of malted milk to improve the taste.

We are close to the International Date Line. St. Lawrence Island sits in the Bering Time Zone, which is about four hours earlier than the Pacific Time Zone. So, we are about seven hours earlier than Detroit.[3]

People in Gambell say that there is a Soviet naval station in the Siberian hills, which we can see across the Bering Sea from our front porch on a clear day. Explosions from there have been so powerful at times that they have rattled windows in the Gambell school. A map of what were described as Siberian slave labor camps appeared recently in *Time* magazine. Two or three of them were not far from St. Lawrence Island. We learned that a prisoner escaped from one of the camps a few years ago and managed to cross the sea to Savoonga.

The winter weather here isn't as cold as it is in the interior of Alaska or in Canada, but at times fierce winds blowing from the North Pole make it bitterly cold. The wind velocity has been recorded as high as 90 miles per hour. Meanwhile, the days are getting shorter. At 4 p.m., the moon may reflect brightly off the Bering Sea, though it isn't dark yet. It is just getting light when I get up at 7:30. Tod must rise to turn on the generator for electricity before I am able to get breakfast. (The generator provides electricity during the day and is turned off at bedtime.)

I'm still trying to find the best way to teach my little children. The school is supplied with a series of elementary-school readers published by Scott Foresman & Co. They include stories about "Dick and Jane,"[4] siblings in a fictional family that includes "Mother," "Father," and a younger sister named "Sally," as well as their pet dog "Spot" and "Puff," their cat. The textbook describes the children visiting a circus and riding a bus. My little ones have no idea what a circus is and have never seen a bus.

The words and stories they introduce for reading are completely foreign to my students in both language and concept. Our children don't have pet dogs. The village huskies are not friendly at all. Best stay away from them. The huskies are working dogs and not fed any more than they need to work. A diet of walrus meat gives them stamina for pulling dogsleds—like filling our cars with gasoline to power them. Dick and Jane's cat, Puff, is an alien creature. I was told that a visiting seaman once left a cat in the village. It did not survive long.

---

3. In 1983, Congress reduced Alaska's four time zones to two. All of Alaska, except for a few far-western islands in the Aleutian Chain, changed to Alaska Time, which is one hour earlier than Pacific Time.

---

4. The Dick and Jane Readers published by Scott Foresman & Co. were widely used in U.S. classrooms for nearly four decades. At the height of their popularity in the 1950s, Dick and Jane helped 80% of all first-graders learn to read. The books described the lives and experiences of a stereotypical American middle-class white family in their suburban home.

Stateside children know basic words like "mother" and "father" and can identity objects in pictures. By contrast, Savoonga children start school with no knowledge of English. I think I am doing fairly well, given this, and considering my lack of training.

I forgot to tell you that I am also the territorial welfare agent. In addition to helping people fill out forms, I am required to investigate applications for assistance and report my findings to territorial authorities.

A recent case illustrates the serious impact that introduction of government-supported financial assistance has had on the traditional values of a community that favors support by extended family members whenever assistance of any kind is required. A new widow with several small children was left with no close male relatives who could support her through hunting or by other means. Her application for financial welfare assistance caused a stir in the community, with some villagers convinced that her in-laws and other extended family members should be required to take care of her family while others in the village supported her efforts to be independent through governmental largesse.

In a lighter vein, if you have no idea what to get us for Christmas, I have a suggestion! We wish we had a fizz bottle to make soda water for Cokes. Alice, the missionary, has one. It would be a treat to have a soft drink occasionally. The bottles are metal and come with carbon-dioxide cartridges. We would be grateful if you sent us the bottle and a couple of boxes of cartridges. Please send by parcel post. We can have the Coke syrup sent over from the Northern Commercial Co. in Nome, as it is cheaper to buy it there than to pay parcel post on it.

Hopefully, the *North Star* will be here in a few days.

Love, Doris

P.S. I imagine you can get a fizz bottle at any large drug store or from a vendor of liquor and bar supplies. In the States, it is used primarily for making soda water for mixed drinks because Coke syrup cannot be purchased except from wholesalers. However, we can buy it because we are outside the continental U.S.

▲ *Marian Waghiyi*

5

The *North Star*

◼

*We have been eating
as much reindeer as we can,
worried that the meat stored in a
locker under the school would
thaw in a warm spell.*

◈ ◈ ◈

▲ *The 5,000-ton government freighter, the* North Star, *delivered supplies once or twice a year to dozens of remote villages on the Alaska coast.*

Sunday, November 4, 1951

Dear Ashfords,

Our supply ship finally arrived—what a madhouse! Imagine unloading, unpacking, and organizing storage for more than $1,000[5] worth of personal groceries, to say nothing of school supplies and food for lunches for the children.

---

5. Worth about $11,600 in 2023 dollars, adjusting for inflation.

▲ *Once ashore, cargo was moved into the village by the women and older children.*

North Star

Perspective: Coastal villages eagerly awaited the North Star

IN THE 1950S, before cargo was carried by air, the 5,000-ton freighter *North Star III* operated by the Alaska Native Service (an agency of the Bureau of Indian Affairs) delivered vital supplies to 40 to 50 villages along the Alaska coast.

While we were on St. Lawrence Island, the freighter made two 10,000-mile round-trips annually during the ice-free months, originating in Seattle. The *North Star* was the third of three vessels, all bearing the same name, that operated for the BIA's Alaska Native Service from 1932 until 1984.

The *North Star* carried food, dry goods, medical supplies, and other necessities for teachers, schools, government agencies, hospitals, and native co-op stores. Typically, the bulkier cargo such as fuel drums, heavy equipment, lumber and construction materials, even small boats were lashed tightly to the deck in the sequential order of delivery. The *North Star* also carried a few passengers who had to have strong stomachs for the sometimes-rough transit to and from shore.

Not completing its annual rounds was not an option for the *North Star,* despite the erratic weather. It was not uncommon for the freighter to take refuge wherever it could from storms, gale-force winds, and rough seas, delaying deliveries to the far north during the short shipping season when the shipping channel was briefly free of ice. In the Arctic Ocean, late in the summer, the captain watched for changes in the weather and kept a close eye on ice floes that had receded. If the wind shifted, blowing the heavy sea ice toward shore, the *North Star's* return route might be closed off before it completed a delivery to Barrow at the northern tip of Alaska.

Arrival of the *North Star* was always a big event in the villages. Transferring cargo ashore was rarely easy as few communities had docks. In places like Savoonga, skinboat crews were hired to lighter the cargo while the freighter anchored offshore. As difficult as this work might be in rough weather, unloading was often even more difficult in other villages.

◀ ▲ *After the* North Star *anchored offshore, skinboat crews were hired to lighter cargo ashore —always an exciting event.*

◀ *Villagers wait to board the* North Star.

Unloading the ship was a major effort. Everyone pitched in. The ship was here for about 12 hours, anchored a half-mile offshore, as the cargo was lightered to shore in skinboats. One man injured his leg when a skinboat overturned during the unloading.

Alice Green and I were kept busy checking the manifests as the women and children carried boxes from the beach to the school and store.

The cargo brought a sudden influx of fresh foods, including eggs, onions, and reindeer meat. The reindeer turned out to be a pleasant surprise. The meat was tender and not at all gamey.

The ship's doctor came ashore to instruct Tod on treatment of various ailments and on administering medications. He also examined villagers with medical problems for whom Tod had been caring. It seems even people with no medical problems came to the clinic to see the doctor. Who can blame them? After all, how often do they get the chance to see a real doctor?

One little girl had just sustained serious injuries from an accidental fall. Two tendons in her hand were severed, and she was unable to control two of her fingers. The doctor performed an emergency operation on the spot as Tod stood by, handing him surgical implements and rushing around looking for sewing needles, silk thread, and more alcohol. Tod dreads having to pull the thread out of the child's hand in a few weeks. Meanwhile, to prevent infection, the doctor instructed Tod to give the little girl penicillin shots daily for four or five days.

The little tyke is only 6. When Tod administered the first shot, he expected screaming and yowling, common reactions among children that age who receive injections—especially in the rear end. But she bared her little rump and climbed up onto a table in the clinic without complaint. Thinking this was too good to be true, Tod proceeded nervously to swab a spot with alcohol and jabbed in the needle. When he was finished, the little girl looked up at him with an angelic smile and said, "Thank you."

Tod gave her the final shot today. He rewarded her bravery with candy from our larder and hopes word will get around the village that children who take their medicine without tears will receive similar rewards.

It is now 3:45 p.m. The sun has set, and it is too dark to continue this letter without lights. This being early November leads us to believe that we will be down to about three hours of daylight at the darkest point in the winter, just before Christmas.

Well, I've run out of material for now, so will try again later.

Love, Doris

❖ ❖ ❖

Dear Mother,

We have been eating well since the *North Star* finally delivered winter supplies on October 31. We are thrilled!

Due to a few shipping errors, we are learning to like—or at least, *tolerate*—several things that one or both of us never have cared for before.

For example, we have a dozen cans of oysters that we did not order. I am no fan of oysters, but I made oyster stew last week. It wasn't bad. We received 500 pounds of flour as well as 300 pounds of sugar—enough to last for two or three years. We also received a case of cake mix, a case of pancake mix, and 20 pounds of biscuit mix. We are well stocked.

I suspect that eventually, when we leave the island, we will be able to sell our surplus food to the store. Jacob Seppilu, the store manager, seems willing to buy almost anything. About half of our oranges were either spoiled or beginning to go bad. We threw away the rotting oranges and offered what was left to the store. Jacob offered us five cents apiece for them and said he could resell them for twice that.

The potatoes survived the trip well, but many onions were spoiled. We also received 30 dozen eggs that must be at least three or four months old, having been in transit since the order was filled in Seattle. The eggs have an odd taste, but none of them was spoiled. I candled them all. But they are beginning to smell somewhat, so I have been making custards, tapioca puddings, and am going to make an angel food cake. Imagine being able to have all the ingredients for an angel food cake right on hand!

We also bought half a reindeer and have been feasting mostly on reindeer steaks and pot roasts ever since. We have been eating as much reindeer as we can, worried the meat stored in a locker under the school would thaw in a warm spell.

When Jacob Seppilu cut the carcass for us, he gave us two hind quarters rather than the usual hind and front quarters. As a result, we have had more than our share of sirloin and round steaks. A few nights ago, we borrowed Alice's meat grinder and made "reinburgers." They were tasty!

We have been using our powdered milk for drinking and find that it isn't too different from fresh milk and certainly is superior to evaporated milk. As I recall, we received 48 cases of Carnation evaporated milk—each case with 24 tall cans.

Our pantry off the kitchen looks like a small grocery store. We have unpacked cases and cases of meats, fruits, vegetables, soups, dried foods, and more. We stored in the attic most of the dry food that won't freeze. Tod climbs up there every week or so to get what we need.

One of the most welcome deliveries from the *North Star* was a mail sack half full of personal letters and business correspondence. We spent an enjoyable evening catching up on news from home. Can you believe, this was the first mail we had received from the States in the nearly two months we have been here?

Thank you for the letters. We hear more are on the way. Evidently the post office in Nome has six weeks' worth of mail for us. We hope it will be delivered next week soon after Alaska Airlines makes its first winter flight to Gambell.

That's all for now. More later.

Love, Doris

❖ ❖ ❖

Dear Glad,

Thanks for sharing the schedule of stage plays to be performed in Detroit this winter. What fun! Our entertainment is closer to home. In the evenings, when our work is done, we often listen to music and programs broadcast on AFRN (Armed Forces Radio Network). A couple of times a week we have dinner with Alice Green and play card games or Monopoly afterward.

Alice is expecting a visitor. A Presbyterian minister, whose luggage includes a turkey, will be traveling to the island from Anchorage to celebrate Thanksgiving. We will have a feast!

We plan to get our school-lunch program under way next week. The village women will take turns preparing the lunches and doing the dishes. I am responsible for the menus. Though uncertain how to prepare menus for feeding 90 students, I will have lots of help. The women have much more experience than I do and are generously willing to share it.

You asked about my household chores. Fortunately, we have a washing machine. When weather permits, we hang the wash to dry on outside clotheslines. When the weather is bad, we hang the clothes in a spacious utility room in the back of the building.

Thankfully, I have help from Ruth Miklahook, a friendly, energetic woman. She was recommended by Alice Green. Ruth bakes bread, cleans our quarters, washes dishes, and does the darning, among other chores. She saves me a lot of work. Last week, after I had left an unusually large stack of dirty dishes, Ruth informed me smugly that she washes her dishes immediately after every meal.

Ruth charges $12 a month. We have not been able to pay her yet, not having received confirmation from Juneau that our paychecks have been deposited into our bank account there. We presume they have, but we would hate to bounce a check.

I have been having a great time the past week preparing all kinds of fancy meals. They have been a treat after the thin diet we subsisted on for almost two months. On Sunday, we had an old-fashioned breakfast of bacon, scrambled eggs, and pancakes. That evening I made a meatloaf with ground reindeer meat, scalloped potatoes, and finished with apple pie. For lunch today, we had cold leftover meatloaf sandwiches, apples, and peanut butter cookies. And tonight, I plan to have pot roast, mashed potatoes, creamed peas, and angel food cake.

Well, I have more letters to finish. A mail plane is due in Gambell this week, so we will send our letters with the mail carrier, Joseph Noongwook, when he goes to Gambell to pick up the incoming mail. Then it will be at least two more weeks before our mail is taken from Gambell to Nome.

Thus, you will always receive letters at least two weeks late—until April. After that, mail deliveries are more irregular because the planes have nowhere to land when the ice on the lake melts. During the summer months, we depend on ships and U.S. Army PBY aircraft.

Well, write soon and often.

Love, Doris and Tod

▲ *Jacob and Myra Seppilu with daughter Nellie and baby.*

6

Village Life

*A dozen or more people
share small one- or two-room homes
with five or six people sleeping
on the floor. Sometimes more than
one family live together*

❖ ❖ ❖

Monday, November 12, 1951

Dear Mother and all,

We experienced a rare occurrence a few days ago that we shall never forget. Shortly before school was to begin, Tim Gologergen came over to tell us that a whale had washed ashore several miles down the beach. Most of the villagers already were headed down to cut it up to feed to their dogs.

We canceled school, and Tim arranged for a couple of the boys to take us on dogsleds to see the whale. We bundled up warmly and climbed onto the sleds, which had no padding because they were to be used to bring whale meat back to the village.

Eager to go, the dogs made a mad lunge over the top of a wooden sidewalk, throwing the sled—and me—into the air. I returned to the sled with a crash. Ouch!

Each sled was pulled by a team of eight to twelve dogs chosen from among about 1,000 dogs that outnumber people about 4-to-1 in the village.

The dogs are Siberian huskies with pale, blue eyes. They are smaller than huskies on the mainland but are just as strong. Most of the St. Lawrence breed came from Siberia originally. They look more like wolves than dogs. And they howl like wolves—especially when they are hungry, which is most of the time during the winter. All but a few of the dogs are tied up at the back of the village not far from the homes of their owners.

When we got to the beach, the men had begun butchering the whale, a small humpback about the size of a station wagon. The villagers thought it had been

▲ *Found washed up on the beach near Savoonga, this big humpback whale stunk to high heaven. The villagers fed it to their dogs.*

killed by a larger orca "killer" whale. In all my life, I have never smelled such a foul odor. The humpback had been dead for about a week and most of the carcass was unfit for human consumption. However, the whale meat provided a good source of dogfood for the village. What a rare experience we shared with the villagers!

We are thoroughly enjoying ourselves here. This afternoon we went for a walk along the seaside. In the distance, about eight miles behind the village, we saw several extinct volcanic hills. The highest of them, we learned, is nearly 2,000 feet. The island is a beautiful place in its own bleak, wind-swept way. There are no trees, and the tundra rolls on for miles. High cliffs overlook the Bering Sea surf roaring onto the black volcanic lava beach.

When everything is covered with a white blanket of snow, the village is much prettier than in warmer weather when the thawed ground turns to mud. Next summer, when we have 24 hours of daylight, we plan to make some overnight excursions.

One of my beginners is a little deaf girl named Erma, the daughter of Edward and Ora Gologergen. She was born without hearing and can't speak well, either. Last year, she was sent to the Washington School for the Deaf in Vancouver,

▲ *The women washed clothes along the rocky seashore.*

Washington. By the time we arrived here for the new school year, however, it was too late to send her for a second year, so she is in my class.

A highly intelligent child, she easily keeps up with class activities and does better schoolwork than most of the children who can hear what I am saying. She can do some lip-reading. But truthfully, she isn't getting much from school. So, I borrowed from her mother Erma's textbooks from Vancouver. After looking them over, I have been giving her special work one afternoon each week.

I am not able to teach her new lessons because I don't know how to teach deaf children. But I am reviewing with her the work she did last year so that when she returns to Vancouver next year, she won't have to start all over again. When she comes to our quarters for after-school work, we have cookies and milk and then go through her books together.

Must close now. Please write soon and often as we look forward to your letters.

Love, Tod and Doris

❖ ❖ ❖

▲ *Snowdrifts and frost obscured the shed of a home where a cold wind blew laundry askew.*

Monday, November 12, 1951

Dear John Charles and Jimmie,

We received your letter, John, and from now on you are not going to be able to shirk your duties as a full-fledged correspondent because of age or size.

When one gets to the point where he can write as nice a letter as you did, then he must take responsibility of *answering* letters. No longer will I be content to hear from your mother about how you are doing. I want to hear first-hand now, hear? Let's see what you can do with pencil in hand, Jim. I'll bet you could give a mean account of yourself, too, if you'd try.

Back to your letter. It might interest you to know that my sixth-graders can't write nearly as well as you boys can. I am having quite a time with them. My fourth-graders are 15 years old on the average. Most of the older boys quit school, and few go beyond sixth grade.

I hope to help my boys improve their English until they can write the essentials, but their main difficulty is they don't speak English anywhere but in school. They know few English words. Also, they haven't seen objects such as trees, cars, and bicycles so they don't know what these things are when they learn the words in reading class.

Don't get the idea that these guys are dumb. They can do a lot of things that would surprise you and Jim. Most of the fellows your ages are good with shotguns and hunt seagulls, cormorants, and other sea birds to help feed their families.

If you could see these villagers' small homes, you would remember how crowded we felt the night I slept with you and Jim up on York Street. A dozen or more people share small one- or two-room homes with five or six people sleeping on the floor. Sometimes more than one family live together.

When I went into a home last week to give a shot of penicillin, I found the mother in bed with four children and six or so other members of the family in the other bed.

Well, I'll close this for now and hope to hear from both of you again. The days are getting shorter, so I should have more time for letter-writing when the temperature drops to 20° below and the sun goes down at 3 p.m.

Write me.

Love, Uncle Tod and Aunt Doris

❖ ❖ ❖

Dear Mother,

The mail carrier hasn't left for Gambell yet, so I'll add a note to the letter I wrote yesterday. I am trying to cook some salmon. Albert Kulowiyi, one of our favorite villagers, brought us a fresh salmon today. I am cooking half of it. Tod froze the other half for later.

I am also making a new scalloped potato dish. I found the recipe in the *Better Homes and Gardens Cookbook.* You add a can of mushroom soup diluted with milk instead of white sauce. I add chopped pimentos and onions. I'm also having corn in deference to Alice, who is coming for dinner. She dislikes fish and will eat only vegetables. I just finished baking a cherry pie and some mincemeat tarts, so I feel I have accomplished a lot this afternoon.

I have bad news. Billy and Virgil, the esteemed houseplants who came with us to Savoonga, have succumbed to the sub-Arctic climate. During a windstorm, a powerful gust blew off a section of the chimney pipe from the living-room stove. A gush of air blew into the room, extinguishing the fire in the stove and spewing oily ash everywhere. The ash would not wash off the plants. Our rescue efforts did not save the African violet and the begonia. Their loss saddened me.

Love, Doris

🔺 *The Kava siblings were the first twins in anyone's recent memory to both survive.*

P.S. November 15. The mail still hasn't gone out, so I'll continue writing. A wind is blowing about 60 miles per hour off the Bering Sea today and, let me tell you, it is mighty cold. During high winds, the stoves don't seem to heat the house because they can't get a proper draft. We are going over to Alice's for dinner tonight and probably will play Monopoly afterward. Brrrr! I hate the thought of going out in that cold.

P.P.S. November 21. The mail STILL hasn't gone out, so I'll add yet another afterthought. No one knows how long it will be before a plane can get over to Gambell as Troutman Lake has not yet frozen solid. A U.S. Army plane recently parachuted supplies for the military and the village, but no one bothered with poor Savoonga. We haven't had any mail since the *North Star* last came, and now we have almost two months of mail piling up in Nome. Once the planes begin to come regularly, however, we expect to get mail in and out every two weeks.

Tomorrow is Thanksgiving. Each year, the villagers organize a dinner at the school. The women prepare the food, and all who come eat together in one of the classrooms, sitting on the floor, as they do at home.

A few nights ago, twins were born with the help of the midwives. Fortunately, there were no complications. Later, the father asked Tod to talk with the ANS doctor about what special care the twins would need. We were surprised, not realizing twins were cared for any differently than a single newborn. The village is buzzing with excitement and some apprehension. These are the first twins in anyone's memory who both have survived childbirth. Everyone hopes they won't die in the next few weeks.

❖ ❖ ❖

Friday, November 23, 1951

Dear Mother,

Well, it is the day after Thanksgiving, and Tod is making me teach today after a week of being sick with a cold. He says I am perfectly all right now and won't listen to my pleas that I am on my death bed.

I do feel much better, though, and have accomplished a great deal this week. I made a pair of socks to give to Alice for Christmas, also a pair of mittens, and I have read several books.

Tod is taking our mail to the post office to have it postmarked, so I'll send this along, too. Of course, the postmark doesn't mean much. We have some outgoing mail sitting over there that was postmarked last month.

We still haven't heard whether we have any money in the bank in Juneau, but we hope to find out when the mail comes. At any rate, we expect to be able to send the money we owe you sometime after the first of the year.

Well, I will close now and hope to have a lot of letters from you if the plane ever gets in with the mail.

Love, Doris

❖ ❖ ❖

November 27, 1951

Dear Mother,

We hear Joseph Noongwook is about to leave for Gambell with the mail, so I'll drop you another quick note.

I have made an inventory of our food supplies that I am sending with this letter so you can see what a long-term food supply looks like. As you will see, we are not doing badly!

In addition to what's on the list, we were able to buy from Alice 20 cans of sliced pineapple, 7 cans of beef gravy, and 9 jars of whipping cream containing a special preservative. We also got 24 cans of ice-cream mix from her and some Hershey chocolate syrup. Alice had received her annual food order in July when the *North Star* made its first visit of the year.

Yesterday, we got a new oil stove made by the Detroit Lubricator Co. It is slightly smaller than the old stove but burns much better. Tod was able to get our kerosene refrigerator working. Now we have ice cubes and can make ice cream. Hurray!

A fierce wind is blowing today. I have no desire to go out. It is only about 4 p.m., but dark outside.

I have no more news. Must close now and get dinner.

Love, Doris

▲ *Tod and I in our new aprons—gifts from Tod's mother.*

Food Order

Perspective: Our grocery order for the 1951-52 school year

THIS HEFTY FOOD order was delivered by the *North Star*:

Apples, 1 case (50 lbs.)

Apples, dried, 1 case (about 10 lbs.)

Apple butter, 1 case

Apple Juice, 1 case

Apricots, canned, 2 cases

Bacon, sliced, 1 case (36 lbs.)

Beef, corned beef hash, 1 case

Beef, roast, 2 cases. Very good!

Beets, sliced, 1 case

Bleach, 1 case

Butter, 3 kegs (100 lbs.)

Candy, hard mixed (25 lbs.)

Carrots, 1 case

Cereal, Post Toasties, 1 case

Chicken, boned, 1 case

Chocolate, ground, 1 case. Makes better cocoa than cocoa powder.

Chowder, clam, 1 case

Cocoa, baker's, 1 case

Coconut, shredded, 1 case

Coffee, 1 case

Corn, creamed, 1 case

Corn, whole kernel, 1 case

Crackers, Graham, 1 case

Crackers, Ritz, 1 case

Crackers, soda, 1 case

Eggs, processed, 1 case (30 doz.) We sold 15 dozen to the store.

Flour (500 lbs.) Enough for about 5 years, we figure.

Flour, cake, 1 case

Frankfurters, brined, 1 case

Fruit cocktail, 1 case

Grapefruit juice, 1 case

Grapefruit, sweetened segments, 1 case. Very good!

Green beans, 1 case

Ham, Hormel (10 lbs.)

Jellies, assorted, 1 case (24 two-pound cans) Enough for 3 years

Jello, assorted flavors, 1 case

Macaroni, Creamette, 1 case

Mayonnaise, 1 case

Milk, malted, Carnation, 1 case

Milk, condensed, sweet, 1 case

Milk, evaporated, large cans, 25 cases

Milk, powdered Klim, 1 case

Milk, powdered skim, 1 case

Noodles, egg, 1 case

Nuts, mixed, 1 sack (25 lbs.)

Oil, Mazola, 1 case

Onions, 1 box (60 lbs.) Most were spoiled.

Oranges, California (75 lbs.) Half were spoiled.

Orange juice, 1 case

Peaches, sliced, 1 case

Peanuts, salted, 1 case

Pears, 1 case

Peas, 1 case

Pineapple juice, 1 case

Plums, purple, 1 case

Potatoes, 2 crates (200 lbs.)

Preserves, assorted, 1 case (24 two-pound cans)

Prunes, dried, 1 box (about 25 lbs.)

Prune juice, 1 case

Raisins, seedless, 1 box (12 cellophane packages)

Sausages, breakfast, 2 cases

Sausages, Vienna, 1 case

Shortening, 1 case

Shrimp, canned, 1 case

Soap, Fels Naptha, 1 case

Soap, Lux, 1 case

Soup, chicken with rice, ½ case

Soup, cream of mushroom, 1 case

Soup, cream of tomato, 1 case

Soup, vegetable beef, 1 case

Soup mix, Lipton's noodle, 1 case

Sugar, brown (50 lbs.)

Sugar, granulated (300 lbs.)

Sugar, powdered (25 lbs.)

Tomato juice, 4 cases

Tomatoes, 1 case

Tuna, 1 case

Vegetables, mixed, 1 case

We also received 29 cases of less-than-case quantities (mostly canned, dried, or powdered) of baked beans, baking powder and soda, cabbage, cherries, catsup, corned beef, corned syrup, cranberries, deviled ham, figs and apricots, honey, kidney beans, butter beans, candy (Hershey and Mountain bars, Snickers, assorted Lifesavers, and gum), various flavors of Jello pudding and pie mixes, lemon juice, lima beans, lunch meat, mincemeat, molasses, olives, oysters, peanut butter, pickles, pimentos, potatoes, salmon, sauerkraut, split peas, sweet chocolate, sweet potatoes, rhubarb, V-8 Cocktail Juice, washing supplies.

7

Mail Anxiety

*This is the longest delay
of mail anyone remembers.
We ordered a canned chicken
from Nome for Christmas,
but it doesn't look like
it will get here.*

❖ ❖ ❖

NOME
Tuesday, December 4, 1951

Dear Mrs. Derby:

This is in reply to your letter of November 30, asking about the mail service from Nome to St. Lawrence Island.

There is a winter plane schedule calling for two trips each month to Gambell; however, this depends on the weather. So far, it has been comparatively mild and the lake at Gambell, which is used as a landing field when it is frozen, must have about eight inches more ice before it will hold the weight of the large planes.

I estimate that the first mail run for the winter will be made within a week or 10 days, and that you should be hearing from your daughter this month. The mail from Savoonga is carried to Gambell by dog team to wait for the plane to Nome.

All mail on hand this summer was dispatched on the *North Star*, which did reach the island, incidentally, with the winter supplies.

Trusting the above information will be helpful, I am
Sincerely yours,
James M. McLean
U.S. Postmaster

❖ ❖ ❖

JUNEAU

Dear Mrs. Derby:

I can well understand your concern at not hearing from your daughter and son-in-law, Mr. and Mrs. Chas. Ray at Savoonga. My family in Wisconsin felt just as you do when I first went to teach in a village on the western Alaska coast.

Mail service in Alaska, especially this time of year, is irregular. Not hearing from them is to be expected, though we know it does cause family concern.

Postmaster John Waghiyi told us mail came by dogsled in winter and skinboat in summer, weather permitting, of course.

Our office would be contacted by radio and advised if the Rays were in any difficulty or serious need. Not having had any such message, we know that all must be well with them. Radio in Alaska is used as people in the States use the telephone.

I was in Nome the middle of October. At that time, the government supply ship, the *North Star*, was at Gambell on St. Lawrence Island, so by now the Rays have their annual supplies.

When I visited Point Barrow, I met some teachers there who had taught for seven years at Savoonga. They loved it and must have found the village to their liking to have stayed as long as they did. They showed me their lovely slides of Savoonga and its people. I am looking forward to visiting there myself.

Here in Alaska, we consider that "no news is good news." I hope this letter will relieve your mind of worry. I am sending a copy of it to Mr. and Mrs. Ray so they will know that we have written to you.

Best regards to you.

Sincerely yours,

(Mrs.) Laura E. Jones

Education Specialist

Alaska Native Service

❖ ❖ ❖

NOME

Dear Mrs. Derby:

I received a copy of the letter written you by Mrs. Laura Jones in our Juneau Office regarding your daughter and son-in-law, Mr. and Mrs. Charles Ray.

You need not worry about them. I talk to Charles over the radio practically every night, and they are getting along in fine shape. One of the reasons you have not heard from them is because the last mail left there sometime in October, and there will probably be no more mail until around the first of January.

Commercial planes cannot land on the island until the ice in the lake at Gambell is 20 inches thick, and so far, it is only about 14 inches.

If you wish to communicate with them in any way, write our office, Alaska Native Service, Box 199, Nome, Alaska. I will be glad to get in touch with Charles on the radio and give him your message. Also, he can be contacted by telegraph, as all messages that come to Nome are transmitted directly to Savoonga by the Army Signal Corps here.

Sincerely,

E. B. Fisher, Administrative Assistant

Alaska Native Service

❖ ❖ ❖

▲ *The children in my classes were all smiles most of the time.*

▲ *The children seemed to be more interested in the language of music than learning English.*

Dear Ashfords,

The poor mail service has drained all inspiration out of me for writing letters, but I'll try anyway. We have received just one batch of mail since we arrived in mid-September, and Lord knows how few of our letters to you have left the island. I imagine the whole family thinks we are dead, but I assure you we are not.

I shall write this in hope it gets out by Christmas, but don't expect a gift until we find out whether we have any money in the bank. You'll probably get Christmas greetings from us about St. Patrick's Day at the rate the mail is moving!

Walrus hunting is starting now as the ice floes move south from the Arctic Ocean. The walruses ride on the moving ice, feeding on clams, soft-shell crabs, shrimp, and other goodies found in shallow saltwater.

In the winter, Arctic winds push the ice floes south into the Bering Sea almost as far as Nelson Island, about 250 miles southeast of us, making ship navigation impossible for all but Coast Guard cutters. In the spring and summer, the ice floes retreat up into the Arctic Ocean.

When the time is right, the men take their dogsleds to the outer edge of the shore ice and launch their skinboats into the open water, which appears when the ice floe moves back a mile or so. You'd have to see the ice formations to understand all this but suffice it to say, everyone in the village has been catching walruses, and there is plenty of fresh meat.

A walrus is larger than a cow and usually has about two tons of meat on it, accounting for a major portion of the villagers' diets. The extremely heavy skin is used in making skinboats.

Making a Walrus Skinboat

▲ Cora Iya

BEFORE beginning the work, the thick walrus hide is scraped clean of hair, muscle, and fat. Then, the hide is soaked in oil to water-proof it. After drying, the inch-thick hide is split carefully and then laid in overlapping sections covering the wooden hull. It is lashed tightly to the frame and stretched tight. The waterproofing must be renewed constantly, and the hulls are recovered completely every few years.

▶ *Facing page top to bottom: Ora Gologergen and Ruth Mikahook positioned a skin; the skin was laced securely to the frame; the heavy skinboats were recovered every few years.*

▲ *Cora Iya split a walrus skin. Sections were stretched over a wooden frame.*

Now I must walk considerably farther out onto the shore ice to empty contents of the chemical toilet. It is considered sanitary to dump sewage far from shore in the Bering Sea, thanks to a strong current and pounding surf that all but eliminates the risk of contamination.

I am working up a Christmas program at school, intending to use all 90 kids. As with school programs everywhere, this is truly a headache. I have never put on a program of any kind. I want to put on a play that I adapted for the north, but the kids have a limited knowledge of English. They speak questions like statements and visa-versa. It doesn't make much difference anyway, since the adults don't understand English well. Yet it is not realistic to expect that I would put on a program in the Yupik language. But I'll figure it out.

We understand Savoonga has a strong tradition of Christmas gift-giving. Typically, families in the village give one gift each, often traditional things, to the teachers. There is widespread trapping of Arctic fox on the Island, and the missionary tells us the teachers always receive a few pelts. If you have suggestions as to what might be done with a couple of white fox pelts, speak up. We may rate a few ivory-carvings, too, given the abundance of walrus and seal on or near the island.

We saw examples of native-carved ivory in Juneau, but most pieces were expensive and priced beyond the usual limits of casual gift-giving. A fancy cribbage board was $65, and watchbands and bracelets ran around $25. I guess if you are a passionate lover of the traditional arts, these prices are not too high to pay for carved ivory.

Except for the government paperwork, my work is going well. I feel I am getting a handle on things and doing less whistling in the dark.

Bye for now.

Love, Tod

❖ ❖ ❖

Thursday, December 20, 1951

Dear Mother,

Like Tod, I lack enthusiasm for letter-writing because we have not received any mail in so long. Everyone in Savoonga is discouraged. This is the longest delay of mail anyone remembers. We ordered a canned chicken from Nome for Christmas, but it doesn't look like it will get here.

Some mail was flown off the island recently in an Army plane, so I hope you have received a bunch of letters. We don't have much news to report.

I have felt more encouraged lately about my teaching. Some of the villagers told Alice we were doing a good job! We are putting on the holiday program next Monday. Then we have a week off. We look forward to relaxing—not that we are killing ourselves with work.

From what we hear, Savoonga is one of the best Alaskan native villages in which to live. The people are kind, thoughtful, and neighborly. And they seem to appreciate us as teachers and neighbors. We feel right at home here.

On Tuesday, the men killed 15 walruses. One of the women brought us some walrus liver. Tod cooked it for himself with onions and proclaimed it to be excellent, a bit like beef liver. I dislike liver but look forward to sampling some walrus meat. if I can get a piece, I am going to try cooking it in the pressure cooker.

Last Saturday, we took a walk out onto the shore ice. All we saw was ice with an occasional patch of water. Although the shore ice is stationary, the floe comes and goes. It was an odd sensation being separated from the ocean by a layer of ice so far from shore. But it is safe. The villagers even take their sleds out onto the ice. We learned that when we walk out onto the ice, someone watches us through binoculars, fearing the shore ice might break off and strand us as it floated out to the sea, or movement of the floe ice might cause the shore ice to buckle. So, rather than cause worry, we have decided not to walk so far out on the shore ice again.

I have a new piece of headgear. Mae Kingeekuk thought I would get too cold wearing just a silk babushka, so she gave me a down-filled, hood-like hat a former nurse had given her that she never had worn. Mae is so motherly and seems to like taking good care of us.

Tod bought a beautiful seal-skin jacket with a hood. It makes him look like an authentic Eskimo. He is quite proud of it. If the mail ever brings my fabric order, I will be able to have my parka made. Tod is waiting for the army-surplus parka he ordered from Nome.

We ordered candy canes for the school children from Sears. However, since the mail hasn't come, I will have to get busy this weekend and make enough popcorn for everyone. We are giving a large can of fruit and some candy and nuts to each family.

The short days continue to amaze us. The sun rises about 10:30 a.m. and sets three hours later. Even on clear days, we seldom see the sun as it shuttles back and forth behind the hills to the south, never rising high enough to see.

I have a little news. We are expecting Grace Crosson, a territorial Department of Health nurse, to arrive about January 1 for a six-month assignment here. We are getting her quarters ready. She will hold a daily clinic in the school. I hope she will be likable and fun as we eagerly anticipate new company.

Will write more later.

Love, Doris

▲ *My new sealskin jacket was a good fit.*

8

Bering Sea Christmas

■

*Christmas is alive and
well in this remote village.
The people are generous
and seem imbued with a
genuine and generous
spirit of giving.*

❖ ❖ ❖

Wednesday, December 26, 1951

Dear Mother and All,

Our second batch of mail FINALLY arrived yesterday and was the most welcome Christmas gift of all. It was our first mail since the *North Star* was here in October.

Before I respond to your letters, I want to tell you about our Christmas.

On Christmas Eve, we put on the annual holiday program. It was a big success judging from the enthusiastic reaction of the villagers. As we've reported, Savoonga has its own custom for the exchange of gifts. Everyone gives something to practically everyone else, and all the gifts—even those exchanged within families—are brought to the school to be distributed after the program.

I spent last weekend making popcorn for the 125 children because, as we feared, the candy canes we ordered from Sears did not arrive. I don't want to see another kernel of popcorn for a long time.

What a fabulous Christmas! Almost every family remembered us in some way or another. We were overwhelmed by their generosity.

I was stunned to receive a wonderful gift from Ellie Alowa, who has become a special friend. Having noticed Tod's hooded, sealskin jacket, Ellie decided to make one for me. However, mine has a white fox trim around the hood and along the bottom. It is beautiful, and I am humbled knowing how long she must have worked on it and the value of the sealskin. When I went over Christmas morning

▲ *The children sang carols at our first Christmas show.*

to thank her, Ellie made me turn around while she pulled and smoothed the jacket, glowing with pleasure.

Mabel Toolie made sealskin *mukluks* for us to match our jackets. We plan to keep the *mukluks* for special occasions. For everyday wear, we will use the boots Mae Kingeekuk made for us. Another woman made Tod a beautiful pair of sealskin dogsled mittens and knitted a second pair to fit inside them for extra warmth. Not to be outdone, her husband gave me a beautifully carved ivory polar bear.

Janet Kingeekuk, the daughter of the woman who is making my parka, gave Tod a pair of fur socks to wear inside his boots. She made me a lovely pair of sealskin-lined house slippers. Helen Pungowiyi made me a pair of house slippers, too. We received about 25 carved-ivory birds as well as carved walruses, seals, and polar bears. Moreover, we were given ivory paperweights; six place-card holders, each with a little bird carved on it; four sets of ivory salt-and-pepper shakers, and two sets of pickle forks.

The crowning touch came after unwrapping the pickle forks when Tod gasped and went into the bedroom to bring out his gift for me. Two pickle forks! We nearly cried with laughter. Christmas is alive and well in this remote village. The people are generous and seem imbued with a genuine and generous spirit of giving.

Mail! Yesterday morning, we were awakened about 9 a.m. The dogsled driver bringing mail over from Gambell had spent most of the night in a severe storm. Imagine the excitement and joy we felt receiving an entire mail sack of letters, magazines, and packages! We spent most of the day reading letters and unwrapping boxes.

Late in the afternoon, we went to the church program where we were given even more gifts. Then, we returned home for our own Christmas dinner. We had ordered a chicken to be flown over from Nome, but evidently the airline lost it, so we feasted on baked ham, sweet potatoes, and several delicious side dishes. Alice, Tod, and I spent a most pleasant evening relaxing after all the excitement of the holidays.

▲ *Joseph Iya conducted the rhythm band.*

This was a day we will never forget. A fierce south wind gusting to 100 mph raged all last night and today. The last thing we wanted to do was go outside. About 1:30 p.m., however, Tod and I went out to carry gasoline from the storage barrels to fill the generators. (Amos Penayah, the custodian, is on vacation this week.) In addition to the high winds, a strong sleet was falling. Imagine sleet stinging your face in a fierce wind.

▲ *My girls looked so pretty in their new holiday dresses.*

December 21 was the shortest day of the year. We look forward to increasing daylight in the coming weeks. We are gaining about five minutes of light per day. Our living room, which is on the northwest side of the school building, hasn't had any direct sunlight for several weeks.

Word has gotten to us through the grapevine that most of the villagers believe we are "good for learning," as expressed by one of the men. Tod and I agree we would much rather make do in Savoonga without modern conveniences, such as plumbing, than teach in a village like Gambell, which has more contact with the mainland and where the people are said to be somewhat self-centered and mercenary.

Savoonga is much like a clan. In fact, three clans are represented in the village. We admire most of the people greatly. And my little children are the cutest things you can imagine! As the missionary said in her welcome speech the day we arrived, Tod and I are lucky to be here.

More later.

Love, Doris and Tod

❖ ❖ ❖

Thursday, December 27, 1951

Dear Mother,

The mail finally came, and we are so happy with our gifts. You could not have picked anything more "divine" than the Divine perfume. I wished for perfume, and I'm glad you selected the kind that won't evaporate easily. The scarf is beautiful.

I have been a little late getting our gifts off but will send them with the next mail. I'm sending a pair of slippers that Janet Kingeekuk made. She said if they were too big for me that I should send them to you. I am sending another pair that Helen Pungowiyi gave me (too small) to Tod's mother. Mae Kingeekuk, Janet's mother, is making me a pair like the ones she made for me to send to Ann McBreen, my college friend. So, I am fixed for slippers!

Glad's gift hasn't come yet but is probably in the mail at Gambell awaiting pickup. There are still several bags of mail there for Savoonga, but there were not enough sleds to carry it all over here in time for Christmas. We will get it this weekend.

Evelyn sent us a landscape painting that she made along with a blue, gray, and white wool plaid shirt from Eaton's. Also, a lot of toys for my children. They will be delighted. Thank you for the toys you sent, too.

Tod's mother and Eunice sent us a box of food—candy mixes, nuts, dates, and all sorts of other goodies. And Ann McBreen sent two large tin boxes of tea cookies from Macy's in New York. Evidently everyone thinks we are starving. The candy you sent from Sanders is the best! We have been gorging on it, and it is almost gone. Alice also gave us two boxes of candy. So, all in all, we fared exceedingly well in the sweets department.

We are expecting a visitor. Dr. Everett Schiller, a researcher with the Arctic Health Research Center in Anchorage, will stay with us for a few days. He is in Gambell now awaiting supplies. His mission is to investigate the mysterious death of more than 40 walruses that washed ashore recently.

According to the rumor mill, some believe the walruses might have died due to exposure to radioactive waste in the Arctic Ocean. One of the villagers told us yesterday that she had heard on the radio that Doctor Schiller is bringing live pigs and rats. A big pork roast would taste mighty good! At any rate, I must fix up the spare bedroom. We have been using it as a storeroom, and it is a mess.

I appreciate so much hearing from you and will try to answer some of your questions.

We receive some excellent radio programs with lots of news and music from the Armed Forces Radio Network. No commercials! We pick up AFRN stations from Fairbanks, Anchorage, Seattle, and San Francisco, to name a few.

Alice Green, the missionary, is a nice woman. To be honest, though, we have grown a little weary of her frequent company. She comes down almost every day. We look forward to the arrival of the new nurse, Grace Crosson, in a week or two. We hope Grace enjoys playing Monopoly; otherwise, she won't have much of a social life.

I have plenty of warm clothes, thank you. The material for my parka came in the mail, and I took it over to Mae Kingeekuk this morning. She will use the wool from two sleeping bags to make the inside of my parka. Mae is going to sew them together for double thickness. Using wool instead of fur will save money. Meanwhile, I am wearing out my old clothes. One pair of slacks has shrunk and no longer fits. So, I gave them to one of the girls who has no mother and whose family is having a hard time. She was so happy that she practically cried. Of course, this made me happy, too.

Everyone seems to be so worried about my bread-making. I have been sent at least six recipes for bread! I hasten to assure everyone that although I do some baking, I am not making my own bread. I have turned that job over to Ruth Miklahook, who makes bread and rolls for us every week.

Your suggestion that I teach Ruth amused me no end. She knows more than I do about so many things. She does all my mending and darning as well as washing, ironing, and other household chores. Her bread is outstanding. She speaks good English and is a charming conversationalist. I can always count on Ruth to share the latest village gossip. I enjoy visiting with her.

By the way, we received the package of books—thank you!

We had to laugh at your question, what do we do on Saturdays and Sundays? Most of the time, we are busier on the weekend than we are during the week. I tidy up the house and write letters and undertake various tasks related to school.

For next year, if we decide to sign up for another year, we plan to order a wider variety of food and more meat, including canned whole chickens. My cakes have been turning out well. I use cake flour and my electric beater. A new oil stove was installed for us a few weeks ago. It is a pleasure to use and cooks reliably. I don't know if I'll remember how to cook with gas or electricity when I get back to the States.

As usual, Tod is hounding me for something to eat, so I guess I'll have to stop and get lunch. He has put on some weight, but not as much as I have.

Love, Doris

❖ ❖ ❖

Your suggestion that I teach Ruth amused me no end. She knows more than I do . . .

Dear Granny,

 Doris seems to have hit the high spots from Savoonga, and I have little else to report. But I did want to say hello and thank you for the nice wallet.

 The villagers have been trooping in all day to get help filling out applications, writing letters, and dealing with tax forms. Maybe I should take some of these forms to school and see if I can teach my older kids to deal with some of the paperwork!

 We are enjoying our break from school. We are keeping busy, but it is nice to leave our routine for a few days.

 I hope your Christmas was as pleasant as ours.

 Write often.

 Love, Tod

❖ ❖ ❖

Dear John Charles and Jimmie,

 We are still impatiently waiting for another letter. Grandma has kept us up to date on your activities, but we haven't heard directly from you in a long while.

 It would be so nice if you could visit us next summer. You would have fun with the Eskimo children. Most of them, especially the older ones, know enough English to be understood.

 Gabriel, a little boy who is about 10, made me a beautiful ivory paperweight for Christmas. He does excellent carving for a boy so young, and I was pleased to have it.

 We have been having a fine time. Now that he has a heavy parka, Uncle Tod hopes to go walrus-hunting with some of the men. More on that later!

 Well, that's all for now. We must hurry over to the post office to mail our letters, as there are several dogsleds leaving tomorrow for Gambell.

 Write us soon.

 Love, Aunt Doris and Uncle Tod

❖ ❖ ❖

Dear Auntie Wun,

I am writing to let you know I am making bread using your recipe.

Usually, Ruth Miklahook makes the bread. However, she is busy cleaning today. At this moment, Ruth is scrubbing the bathroom floor while singing hymns at the top of her lungs. She says my dough looks well-prepared, and I am almost ready to pop it into the oven.

Ruth is such a good worker; I don't know what I'd do without her. In addition to everything else, she is even making me a pair of curtains for the bathroom.

We had an accident last week caused by the weather. A strong east wind came up in the night and wreaked havoc with the kitchen and living room stoves. The next morning, we found a layer of soot a quarter-inch thick over everything in the two rooms. Luckily, Tod had gotten up in the night and turned the stoves off to prevent fire. We had to cancel school. With Ruth's help, it took us most of the day to get the place in livable condition again.

In the meantime, Tod and several men from the village discovered part of the chimney pipe had blown completely off, creating a funnel for the wind that had blown down and fanned the fires. Tod cleaned the stoves completely and arranged for the chimney to be repaired. The stoves have both been working well ever since.

Tod and I have plenty of warm clothes. We both have our sealskin jackets for fall and spring. To venture out in the coldest weather, Tod bought an alpaca-lined army parka from the army surplus store in Nome. It just arrived. One of the women is going to sew fur around the face of the parka to protect against the wind.

The material for my parka came, too. In a week or so I will be all set. I am wearing out all my old slacks and sweaters as well as some of Tod's old sport shirts. Tod and I both have fur socks to wear inside our *mukluks* when we go outside. We always stay warm.

Tod hasn't gone walrus-hunting yet, though he has ventured out with his .22 rifle to take pot shots at birds. He may go soon. Tim Gologergen promised Tod he would take him seal- and walrus-hunting as soon as Tod's new alpaca parka arrived. Tod is eager to go. Of course, he won't be able to shoot anything big with his .22. Likely he either will borrow a gun from one of the men or go along just to help with the skinboat.

There are few fur-bearing animals on the Island except for the Arctic foxes and seals, and even the local seals don't have the high-quality fur used to make seal coats. That species is found farther south near the Pribilof Islands.

Cousin Bobby would have a fine time up here with the village boys about his age to take him bird-hunting. They shoot seagulls with sling shots, and often come by the school with a brace of birds. This usually occurs in the summer and fall. The villagers seem to like seagulls and cormorants, but most non-natives don't care for fishy-tasting seabirds.

By the way, there is no need to send packages by air mail. Just send them by regular parcel post. The parcel post mail goes to Seattle or Vancouver, British Columbia, by train and then by sea to Seward, Alaska. From there, it is moved on the Alaska Railroad to Anchorage, from which it is flown to Nome and from there over to St. Lawrence Island.

Parcel post takes a little longer, but the delay doesn't matter much because our mail deliveries are so irregular anyway.

We are constantly in awe of the forces of nature we witness on the Bering Sea. When the floe ice came down from the Arctic through the Bering Strait, it brought with it icebergs that looked like ships on the horizon. The shore ice that had formed for about a half-mile out from the beach has mostly melted, though some high piles of ice surrounded by water look like icebergs.

Your remark about trimming an evergreen tree for Christmas was amusing. We have not seen a single tree on the island. The only wood here is either driftwood or lumber shipped in from the States. Few of the villagers have ever seen a green tree, making it hard to teach the little children about such things in their readers.

The villagers are open and friendly. They have a rich culture and a deep sense of humanity. Everything is shared. There is meat for every family in the village, even if some of the hunters don't bring home a walrus. The old people are always taken care of, so there is no need for help from outsiders. Indeed, only a few of the old people have applied for government benefits.

Everyone seems to have a wonderful sense of humor, too. Even my little children love to tease me. Their initial shyness seems to have worn off.

The villagers have an unusual custom of giving away their children to one another. There are no orphans here. Adoption is common. I believe this is because every family needs menfolk to hunt for food. The people have a custom of naming their children for someone who has died. A family suffering the loss may claim that child at any time.

We wondered why parents would name children in this way, given the risk of someone claiming their child. The only explanation we could imagine is that naming a newborn is the best way of paying tribute to someone who has passed away. They all love their children dearly, yet will allow even non-natives to adopt them so long as the children are not taken off the island.

You asked about how the people live. I have visited quite a few homes. Aside from obvious differences, families here are not so unlike those in the States. The family works together, cares for one another, and everyone has responsibilities.

Sometimes two or more families live together. Some homes are clean. Others not so much so. Just like in the States.

Ruth Miklahook's home and children are spotless. I enjoy visiting her and several other women. I look forward to days like today when we work together.

I often play outside with my little children after school and sometimes invite them into our home for tea parties with cookies and fruit juice. Tod says I've finally found some friends on my own level. It's true, I have much fun with the little ones as we sit in a big circle on the floor and jabber to each other—mostly in Yupik.

Most of the villagers speak some English. A few speak it fluently. The people on our Island speak a dialect that is much like that spoken in Siberia. That's where the Yupik people came from. Many have relatives living just across the strait. However, no one from St. Lawrence has visited their Siberian families for more than a decade, since before the start of World War II.

The native population in Siberia was being subjected to political propaganda,

Cold War

Perspective: Siberian visits forbidden during the Cold War

THE YUPIK ESKIMO people are believed to have lived along the Bering Sea in eastern Siberia and on Alaska's southwest coast and sea islands, including St. Lawrence Island, for at least 10,000 years.

For most of this time, the Yupik people were free to travel for trading and family visits back and forth across what became the international boundary separating Siberia from Alaska.

That freedom was abruptly taken away when the border was closed in 1948 by the U.S. and the Soviet Union as the Cold War between the two nations intensified. It was still closed when we taught school in Savoonga. Many of the islanders knew people and had relatives on the other side of the International Date Line.

Given its proximity to the Soviet Union, just 36 miles away, St. Lawrence Island became an important defense site and listening post during and after the war. The U.S. Army and Navy developed radar, sonar, and communications facilities in Gambell to monitor the Russians. The Civil Aeronautics Authority constructed buildings and lodging to support its own operations.

Though we lodged two intelligence officers from the Air Force for a time and heard occasional rumors about Russian military activity on the distant Chukchi Peninsula, we did not know the full extent of what the U.S. military was doing on the island. Its intelligence-gathering activities were supposed to be secret.

While we were in Savoonga, the Air Force was building an early-warning radar site at its new Northwest Cape Air Force Station. Many of the men from the village made good money working on the construction project.

and the St. Lawrence Islanders didn't like it turned on them. The Siberians tried to convince the St. Lawrence Islanders that the communist system is superior to our democratic republic, boasting that their every need was being provided by the Soviet government. The islanders weren't buying it. The international border has been closed by both governments.

Homes in the village are made of wood—small frame huts. Most are one-room affairs with at least one and often two or three sheds in front where they keep their newly killed birds, seals, and walruses. The odor in the sheds is dreadful. Their dogs are tied up nearby. Nearly every home has a radio, and the people listen religiously to Tod's morning and evening broadcasts to the mainland.

Despite its remote location, Savoonga is one of the most advanced Eskimo villages in Alaska. Among other things, the villagers have their own light plant, which is run as a non-profit cooperative. The monthly cost of operating the plant is shared by everyone using it.

The weather here doesn't get too cold. When it does get cold—anywhere below zero—it's a dry cold and the wind doesn't blow. We feel the cold more intensely at 20° above zero with a stiff wind. Some of the north and east winds seem to blow right though you, and the south wind we had on Wednesday was so strong that we couldn't have had school even if we had not been on vacation.

Mrs. Alowa, who made me the sealskin jacket, asked last night what rats and pigs look like. Do they have fur? We have lemmings here, rodents that are cousins to rats and mice, but they haven't bothered us.

By the way, I just took the bread out of the oven, and it turned out just right. Tod, Ruth, and I sampled my rolls happily. So, I guess I CAN bake after all! By the way, I was glad to receive your recipe for baked beans, as we have dried beans in storage.

Speaking of which, I must get busy with dinner. Will write again soon.

Love, Doris and Tod

We feel the cold more intensely at 20° above zero with a stiff wind.

9

Windy Winter

Because of the cold spell,
we haven't attempted to heat the back end
of our quarters today. The current
temperature in the bedroom
is 10° above.

❖ ❖ ❖

Saturday, January 5, 1952

Dear Mother,

I am dashing off a quick note as the mail plane will probably come over to the island next Tuesday, and some of the men are going over to Gambell with the outgoing mail if it is a nice day.

After a mild fall, the weather has become much colder. Tonight, it is about -6°, and the wind makes it seem much colder. But I'm all set for winter. Mae Kingeekuk finished my parka this week. It is toasty warm and so pretty. I'll have Tod take a photograph of it. It is made of a soft scarlet flannelette decorated with figures of skiers and black fir trees printed on it. We also have some heavy ski pants that the government

◄ *I was warm in my new parka.*

87

▲ *The children erected a snowman next to the school.*

provided, so we are warm when we go outside. The women all tell me I look like a real Eskimo. And when the children see me, they all say, "Caw, Caw!", which is Yupik for "Oh, look!"

Our kitchen drain has frozen, and Tod is thawing it with a welder. I just went into the bedroom to get some Kleenex. Because of the cold spell, we haven't attempted to heat the back end of our quarters today. The current temperature in the bedroom is 10° above.

We will sleep tonight on our new sofa-bed in the living room. Even the chemical toilet in the bathroom has frozen solid. However, the living room and kitchen are warm, and the rest of the house is usually warm enough except when we are slammed with an icy wind.

We are teaching again after last week's break. The village put on a celebration on New Year's Day with all kinds of athletic events, a tug-of-war, and even a dogsled race that Tod judged.

We spent most of our vacation answering mail and filling out forms from Juneau. It was a nice break from teaching.

I'm getting a lot more out of my children, and so is Tod. We are feeling even more encouraged.

That's all for now. Write often.

Love, Doris

❖ ❖ ❖

Dear Mother,

My, what a long list of questions you sent. I'll try to answer some of them.

Yes, our financial worries have eased, but we must save enough to pay cash in advance in a few months when we place our grocery order for next year. Federal Civil Service employees recently received a raise, which we did not know was coming, so we were surprised and delighted when we saw our bank statements.

Your worries about the skinboats are misplaced. They are incredibly strong, and the men are excellent sailors. The only accident we know about occurred years ago when a hunter attached a hemp rope to his harpoon instead of a skin rope. When the harpoon struck the walrus, the man's hand became tangled in the rope. He was pulled over the side of the skinboat when the walrus pulled away and dove into the sea. That was the last ever seen of the man.

Anyway, if Tod goes hunting, likely he will not do any shooting. His rifle is too small. So, he'll probably just take photos.

You asked about Alice Green. She's 35, a frustrated old maid from Denver. Truthfully, though Alice is good-hearted, we've grown weary of her. Alice is a know-it-all who tries to run everybody's business—most of all, ours! She is an authority on ALL subjects. She has been here five years and knows everyone's business, inside and out. She isn't particularly religious, despite being a Presbyterian missionary, and there is a movement afoot to have her transferred. Alice spends most of her time reading, and the villagers regard her as lazy. We do, too.

Alice has done some nice things for us, and if we didn't have to see her so often, the situation would be different. But she is here all the time and tries to run the school. She dislikes Tim Gologergen, our teacher-aide, and never misses an opportunity to say something nasty about him. She also disliked the last teachers, mainly because they wouldn't allow her to run things. We try to stay on her good side, but this has become increasingly difficult.

Don't send any more dolls, as we have three that we can dress and play with. A school in Oakland, California, sent us two cartons of gifts. They arrived after Christmas, so we are saving them for next year.

Tod has made some corner shelves for our ivory birds and animals. We enjoy work that went into carving them. My favorite is a lovely little seal that one of my students made for me. It was artistic work!

▲ *Seal carving. My Christmas gift from Gabriel.*

The wind is blowing hard tonight. I dread going outside, but I told Tod I would accompany him on his medical calls. The temperature was 30° above today, so it is relatively warm—if only the wind would die down.

Dr. Schiller, the health researcher, arrived Friday and left Monday afternoon. He was here to investigate the unexplained walrus deaths and to conduct his research into a disease found among the dogs of St. Lawrence Island. The latter is called a "hydatid" disease, which is carried by tapeworms and can be transmitted to humans.

No, I can't speak any Yupik, though Tim has taught us a few words.

The $1,200 allocated for books include all textbooks, workbooks, and library books. As you know, we teach with the *Dick and Jane* series and are sent new workbooks for this series each year. I am using the pre-primers with my beginners, and the *Look and See, Work and Play,* and *Come and Go* books with my first-graders.

I recently received a teachers' manual for a new series, *We Talk, Spell, and Write* for a basic language program. I want to get some workbooks for next year, as the students already know the Dick and Jane characters. However, I am basing much of our reading on classroom conversations about experiences they understand. The children draw pictures illustrating the conversations, then we make books out of their pictures with the words printed underneath.

Mae Kingeekuk was concerned that the new parka Tod ordered from Nome would not be warm enough because it didn't have fur on the hood around the face. So, she found some fur and sent one of her girls over to get his parka. We slipped it out of the house without Tod knowing.

That evening, Mae and her husband, Theodore, brought it back. Tod was so happy with it, and of course Mae was pleased, too. She refused to accept any payment.

Time is going by so quickly. The school year will be over before we know it.

Well, Tod is worried about getting over to see his patients, so I'll close for now. Write soon.

Love, Doris and Tod

❖ ❖ ❖

Dear Glad,

Our Christmas bounty seems endless!

Your package didn't arrive until last week. Having another parcel to open gave us much pleasure. We also received a big box from Tod's brother Burton and his wife in Nebraska. Inside we found all kinds of jellies, a fruit cake, nuts, marshmallows, three pounds of pitted dates, fudge, and even a little artificial Christmas tree.

I'll try to answer your questions. The villagers live in small frame houses with a few pieces of furniture and coal stoves for cooking and heating. They keep their homes much cooler than we do. The people usually sit on the floor, and many of the poorer families sleep on the floor, too.

Some villagers speak good English considering that many of them have had no formal schooling. No, the Eskimos on St. Lawrence Island do not live like those you read about in books. Our villagers have never seen an igloo. Yes, they eat whale meat when they can get it, but the Savoonga villagers here don't hunt for whales like the folks in Gambell. They have electric lights just like you have.

We were disappointed that our sun-tan bulb was broken. We are thinking of ordering another one from Sears, which guarantees their packing. Our quarters are heated by oil stoves. Each school room has a stove, and there is another one in the utility room.

Yes, the federal government supplies food for school lunches. A special kitchen is housed in little building about 100 feet from the school. We serve soup, beans, macaroni and cheese, cereals, scrambled eggs, and all sorts of other things.

The children are finally past their shyness. In fact, they have become talkative. We seldom have discipline problems. Anything serious is referred to the welfare committee, a committee of the Village Council, to decide punishments. For example, quite a few older children were coming to school late every day. Tod would keep them in at recess, but that punishment didn't seem to faze them. So, after discussing the problem with the welfare committee, it was decided that any child who came late or who otherwise misbehaved would have to stay after school and scrub the school walls and floors. Since then, few children have been late.

Some children are smarter than others, just as in classrooms everywhere, but most pick up things quickly. We don't have a set procedure for advancing the children. We move them up to the next grade when we think they are ready.

No one will play canasta with me! Alice doesn't feel she can play cards in front of the villagers because they might think she is gambling.

We are showing movies that we received in the mail. One film is about the 1943 World Series, another is about the Havasupai Indians in Arizona, and a third is about gray squirrels. They are educational films for the school children, but everyone in the village wants to see them. So, we scheduled separate showings for the women and men this evening as none of the classrooms is large enough to hold everyone at one time.

Well, I must begin dinner. Write often.

Love, Doris and Tod

❖ ❖ ❖

Thursday, January 17, 1952

Dear Eunice and H.F.,

After three months of infrequent and irregular mail, the delivery of letters every two weeks feels like a luxury. We appreciated your news reports but were amused by your efforts to keep us up to date on world events.

We pick up all sorts of radio stations on our new Zenith Transoceanic radio and listen to news from the Armed Forces Radio Network several times a day. The station with the strongest signal is Radio Moscow, which booms in with frequent English programs reporting the real lowdown about what we capitalists are doing. We were amused by the propaganda at first, but it became monotonous. Generally, we stay tuned to AFRN from Nome.

As Pappy guessed, teaching is difficult when the students and teacher do not share a common language. Truthfully, the result is pretty much what he said—we are not getting through to them too well. I tried to expose them to a few practical skills, such as how to use a mail-order catalog.

It's a struggle! I'll keep plugging, though I sometimes wonder if it's worth it.

Juneau instructs us as to what teaching methods to use. These methods just about jive with what we are doing, so perhaps we expect to do too much.

Doris's children tease her a lot and have a great time. When she held up a picture of an owl yesterday, a chorus of little voices informed Doris it was an *aneepa*, which is Yupik for owl. Then they howled with laughter. Doris seems to be picking up as many Yupik words as they are learning English words. If we stay long enough, we all may have a common language.

On a more serious note, several dogsleds are going over to Gambell with three TB patients as soon as the weather clears. From Gambell, they will be flown to Nome and then on to Sitka, in the Alaska Panhandle, where they will be admitted to the Mt. Edgecombe Hospital.

It is pitiful and tragic that these villagers must leave home because I'm told that no one taken to a mainland hospital with TB ever returns. A lump comes to your throat seeing the families dress the kids in their Sunday best and send them off.

Two of the three patients are young, so maybe they will have a better chance of recuperating than the older ones. One youngster, Morris Toolie, is about 20. One of his lungs is gone. Despite our hopes, we fear the young man won't live much longer. Another young patient is a 16-year-old girl who cried when we told her a hospital bed was available. Her father had TB, too. He was taken away last spring and died in the fall.

We are expecting the new territorial Department of Health nurse to arrive sometime this month, at which time my medical role will end for a spell. She will spend six months in Savoonga and then six months in Gambell. We expect to have her until June. Our fervent hope is that that she will be compatible. Being a Monopoly player will help.

I'm out of news, so I'll stop for now. More later.

Write often.

Love, Tod and Doris

❖ ❖ ❖

Monday, January 21, 1952

Dear Mother,

A short note.

We have had high winds the past eight days. They were so powerful today that we cancelled classes. Weather forecasters in Gambell said the strongest gust was 93 mph. That was the maximum velocity that the station's instruments could measure!

I gave my first shot of penicillin last week to the 3-year-old adopted son of Amos Penayah, our custodian. Amos is such a sweet old man. He reminds me of granddaddy. Amos was the first herder on the island when the reindeer were brought over from Lapland.

Love, Doris

▲ *Elders Logan Annogiyuk and Amos Penayah, our custodian, in their reindeer parkas.*

❖ ❖ ❖

Saturday, February 2, 1952

Dear Mother,

This is the first chance I've had to get a letter off to you. You will not have heard from me for about a month because the last plane into Gambell failed to take our outgoing mail back to Nome. It is still in Gambell and will go out on the next plane along with even more mail coming from Savoonga.

This week has been hectic. A flu epidemic swept through the village. Gambell got it first, and then the people who went over to pick up the mail brought it back with them. We cancelled school all week.

I don't believe there was a single family that didn't have someone who was sick last Sunday. It took us more than six hours to visit everyone.

I have become competent giving penicillin shots. The flu was not too serious, but many villagers got colds of top of it. Tod got a bad cold, too, and had to spend most of the week at home. He is a lot better now but is taking it easy until school resumes next week. Surprisingly, I didn't catch anything as I certainly was in contact with enough germs.

Alice is going to Gambell for a few weeks, so I am having her over for dinner tonight. I am making ice cream, her favorite dessert. The weather has been relatively warm the past few days. The temperature dropped to zero today though the sun is shining brightly. The days are getting much longer now. The sun goes down about 4 p.m. and comes up about 9 a.m.

The nurse is supposed to come on the next plane into Gambell. I wish she had come on the last one. We could have used her last week. We heard gossip about the nurse from a visitor last week. (It seems we are expected to offer lodging and meals to any non-native visiting the village.) The woman sounds like a real character. The pilot said she is an immense woman who has been a nurse for many years. If she really is big, she may have difficulty getting into some of these homes as many of the doors are so narrow that I have trouble getting inside. We have been busy fixing up the nurse's quarters. She will reside in the old schoolhouse.

Tod has been taking a ribbing since a pamphlet arrived in the mail addressed to the "Superintendent of City Schools, Savoonga, Alaska." He is proud of the fact that he is already a superintendent at age 23.

The girls in my sewing class are making parkas for our dolls. I will send you one when they finish. I've asked them to bring scraps of fur from home to make boots and mittens and trim for the parkas.

Yes, we finally received a notice that we have money in the bank. We want to have enough to buy our groceries in April for next year. We want to pay cash to save money as there is a 14% carrying charge for credit. We will need to order

▲ *Nurse Grace Crosson joined us for dinner to celebrate Tod's birthday.*

only about $500 worth of food, as so much of the food we ordered this year will be left over. I want to order another frozen chicken from Nome for Tod's birthday next month. We so enjoyed the last one, and we've almost decided it is worthwhile to spend the extra money occasionally to get something fresh.

You asked about my schoolroom. It has little chairs, and I have arranged the desks into tables instead of lining them up in rows. I think the little children are better off at tables. I have four children at most tables and two tables with five kids. I wish you could come and see them. I am amazed at how fast they are learning English. Many of the mothers have noticed, too.

Tell your friend Irene that there are Catholic missionaries on King Island and Little Diomede Island. About 50 years ago, when the first missionaries came to Alaska, the Territory was divided among the various denominations. St. Lawrence is Presbyterian. The missionary on King Island is Father Tom Cunningham, a Catholic, whose life was dramatized on NBC Television not long ago.

One of the older girls at school wrote down an Eskimo story her grandmother used to tell and gave it to me. That got Tod and me started on the idea of collecting Eskimo stories from the older people and writing them down in English for the children to read. We have even thought of making a book out of them. The first big project, however, is to hear the stories and get them down on paper.

No, I never use tablecloths, except when we have company. We have bright red oilcloth on the kitchen table. It makes a cheery table cover.

As I look out the window, I see a beautiful sunset behind the hills in the southwest. It is just 4 p.m.

Well, bye for now.

Love, Doris and Tod

February 27, 1952

Dear Mother,

The nurse finally arrived. She is almost as tall as Tod and, I suspect, weighs about 250 pounds! I cringe every time she sits down on one of our chairs for fear it will break. She will be here for about three months, then go to Gambell for three months.

I went over to Alice's quarters today and helped myself to some of her books. She is due back from Gambell next week. While there, the Civil Aeronautics Authority (CAA) plane arrived to stock the agency's people with fresh and frozen foods. The CAA is able to operate a frozen food locker because it has electricity 24 hours a day. Alice knew the supply flight was scheduled, so she wired a CAA friend in Anchorage, asking her to send a case of frozen peas, broccoli, strawberries, and orange juice and lemonade concentrate. Then, she traded some of the broccoli for a few servings of beef. She said she would send it over on the first dogsled leaving for Savoonga. We can hardly wait! Alice said we could go ahead and eat some of it.

Grace Crosson, the nurse, holds office hours every day in the school clinic. She practically lives with us. She is quite nice, though moody. On her first day, she came over to work in the clinic and left just as my little children were coming in from recess. Grace stands out in her red parka trimmed with wolf fur. When I returned to the classroom, the children were crowded at the window watching the new nurse. One of the more precocious little rascals announced, "There goes Santa Claus!"

I have had Grace over for dinner several times already, as she usually visits us every day.

Well, must close now. Will write again as soon as I get some mail to answer.
Love, Doris and Tod

Grace stands out in her red parka trimmed with wolf fur. . . . One of the more precocious little rascals announced, "There goes Santa Claus!"

▲ *Richard Alowa and the "aneepa" (an owl).*

P.S. February 29. Grace noticed a little owl sitting in the doorway of her shed. All the children gathered around until the little bird was so frightened it didn't know what to do.

We decided to keep him for the children. First, we put him in a box and brought him home. Amos, our custodian, made the owl a little house with chicken wire around it. We covered it with netting. We are using a couple of toy dishes for his food and water.

I don't know whether the owl will survive. If he doesn't, Albert Kulowiyi wants to skin him and send him to the Denver Museum of Natural History. Albert collects specimens on the island for the museum.

The children are all so excited. The Yupik name for owl is *aneepa*. I knew this word because earlier, when I showed the little children a picture of an owl, *aneepa* was the word they used.

By the way, will you send me a package with some of my music?

1. Hanon (exercises)

2. A sheet of arpeggios

3. Fifty-Nine Famous Pieces (the book I used)

4. Jerome Kern Favorites

I promised Alice I would help some of the girls with their music, so having this music will allow me to prepare myself by practicing an hour a day on the piano at the church.

Love, Doris and Tod

▲ *Fred Okungmiliak returned after a successful seal hunt.*

10

Icy Spring

◾

The bathtub drain is frozen.
I'll be happy when it thaws
so we can heat water on the
stove and take real
baths in the tub.

❖ ❖ ❖

Wednesday, March 5, 1952

Dear Mother,

Alice returned from Gambell on Monday with Rev. Rolland Armstrong, who oversees the Presbyterian missions in Alaska. He will be here a week, staying with us. Alice returned with the first-class mail, which was most welcome as we hadn't had any mail at all for three weeks due to bad weather.

The village held a reception for Rev. Armstrong. Afterward, he, Alice, and Grace Crosson, the newly arrived nurse, came to our place for dinner. Tod and I jumped into our mail right afterward while our guests washed the dinner dishes.

I must admit, we have an easy teaching schedule. School begins at 9 a.m. At 10:15, we have a 15-minute recess during which Tod and I return to our quarters for a second cup of coffee while the students play outside or go home for a bathroom break. My little ones go out to the kitchen for lunch at 11 a.m. Tod's students eat about 11:40, and then we are free until 1 p.m. School ends about 3:30, although we always have piles of paperwork.

Hundreds of government forms must be filled out. A recent one wanted to know how we spent our free time when we were not teaching. The question angered Tod, and he told me to tell them we spend most of our time filling out damned government forms. I didn't say that. Instead, I told them what they wanted to know.

Now, as to your questions about the village. At present, we can't see the Bering Sea. It is covered with about five feet of ice and snow as far out to the horizon as we can see. In the summer, when the weather is clear, it is often blue on sunny days.

The villagers prefer meat. Walrus is their favorite, with seals and birds coming in second. They eat the birds raw, and I feel ill watching someone suck the bones. In the summer, they eat fish. A limited choice of food can be purchased at the store.

A few berries can be found on the island. We don't eat them because the dogs wander all over and carry a disease caught from foxes that can be passed on to humans, seriously affecting the liver. This is why we haven't adopted a puppy. I had hoped Alice might bring back a kitten for us when she returns from visiting Fairbanks in the spring. But on second thought, I realized this was not a good idea. The dogs would likely kill it.

The students have milk at school, and some of the more prosperous families buy milk to drink at home. Currently, most of the villagers' income is from working for a construction company that is building a radar station at Northeast Cape. The contractor pays fabulously well—$2.75[6] an hour for laborers. Many villagers have made between $2,000-3,000[7] in a summer.

The villagers also trap white fox to sell their pelts, carve ivory for cash, and earn money for lightering of ships that unload here. Most of the villagers are well-to-do these days, but evidently are not saving for the future when the work at Northeast Cape is completed. We are trying to find out from the BIA in Juneau about savings plans.

We saw the Northern Lights for the first time Monday night. They were greenish and beautiful.

Love, Doris

P. S. We got some charming letters for the children from a school in Minnesota. They were studying Eskimos and looking for pen pals. The teacher had written to the BIA and was given our names and address. One of the most common questions was, "Do you live in igloos?" In his reply, Joseph Pungowiyi, one of Tod's precocious students, responded, "No, you silly boy! We live in houses—just like you." That response has become our little joke.
"Tod, have you emptied the chemical toilet?"
"No, you silly girl, I'll do it later!"

❖ ❖ ❖

---

6. The U.S. minimum wage in 1951 was 75 cents an hour.

---

7. The equivalent of about $25,000 to $34,000 in 2023 dollars, adjusting for inflation.

Sale of Fox Pelts Was a Source of Cash Income

▲ ▲ Thalia Sevouhok and Lynn Pungowiyi proudly display an Arctic fox caught on a trapline.

▲ Ora Gologergen skinned a fox while her children, Arnold and Marilyn, looked on.

◀ The native co-op store paid trappers $6 each for prime pelts.

Saturday, March 8, 1952

Dear Mother,

Today is windy, though the temperature has risen to about 33°. We are going to Alice's for dinner. We take turns hosting dinner on Saturdays. We are going to have a REAL beef steak that she brought back from Gambell! Alice is going out to a church meeting in Fairbanks in April, so probably will bring more fresh food back with her.

Last night, a baptismal service was held at church. It was so sweet! All the babies and small children were dressed up with their hair slicked down. They are such darlings.

The other day, Tod took a photo of one of our favorite little tykes—Lawrence Stanley Kingeekuk, the one-year-old grandson of Theodore and Mae Kingeekuk. His mother has made him a toddler-sized pair of sealskin pants just like the hunters wear. He also has a tiny pair of high sealskin boots, and his mother, Margaret, turned his parka inside out so the fur would show. The charming baby had his usual quizzical expression. I hope the photos turn out well.

Our plumbing pipes are completely frozen. Consequently, we haven't had a real bath (in the bathtub) in several months. We must rely on "spit baths"—using a basin of heated water.

I must stop because Tod wants me to wash his hair. He washed mine earlier today. We help each other due to lack of running water.

It is such an ordeal having Tod wash my hair that I'd almost rather leave it dirty. As he stands over me while I'm rubbing in the shampoo, Tod trickles cold water down my back. He enjoys his little prank. Then he pours ice water over my head and generally has a great time. When I protest, he says he gets bored and must amuse himself in some way.

I'm going to get even this afternoon when it's my turn to "help" Tod.

I also must cut Tod's hair, but I am a poor barber. We have clippers, but I can't seem to manage them. Tod is not appreciative of my efforts and plans to ask Tim to take over the barber job—a change for which I will be quite grateful!

Love, Doris

❖ ❖ ❖

Our plumbing pipes are completely frozen.

Dear Mother,

Yesterday was Tod's birthday, and what a surprise it was. He received so many gifts! I gave him a walrus-intestine raincoat, made like a parka and trimmed with birds' feathers. What a sight! One of the old women made it. Few women know how to make raincoats in the old way. After the villagers encountered outsiders, they began to substitute manufactured fabric for walrus intestine.

I also gave Tod a pretty, white sealskin belt with an ivory buckle made by one of my friends, Katherine Noongwook. But she embroidered little flowers on it, and it looks rather feminine. So Tod gave it to me. It will look pretty on a white dress.

Alice gave him a box of

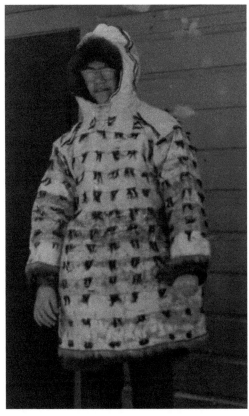

▲ *Tod looked handsome in his walrus-intestine snowshirt, a traditional Eskimo raincoat.*

candy, and Grace gave him a beautiful pair of wool socks, which I suspect someone had made for her. Janet Kingeekuk gave him a fossil-ivory artifact, an old harpoon head that her brother had polished. She also gave him a darling little ivory brooch in the form of a man about an inch high. Her brother made it, too. I told Tod it would look nice on some of my suits, and now he suspects me of conspiring to steal his gifts.

Katherine Noongwook's little girl, Martha Jane, who is just a year old, gave Tod an Eskimo yo-yo. Katherine is about my age, and a good friend. The yo-yo is made of fox paws on strings balanced in the middle with an ivory button. The object is to get both paws spinning in a circle in opposite directions at the same time. There is a trick to it, and I haven't mastered it yet, but Tod has been practicing for days and gotten the hang of it.

David Seppilu, one of his older students, gave him an exquisite little carved bird. Ora Gologergen's little girls gave him a handsome billfold. Tod was surprised that so many people remembered him.

For Tod's birthday dinner, we had a beef roast that Alice brought back from Gambell. It was delicious! I roasted potatoes in the same pan and served creamed frozen peas. For dessert, I made an angel food cake covered with a gooey, white frosting that I made with my electric mixer. I must say, the cake was perfect. I had brought some birthday candles with me to Alaska but had no candle holders, so I used Life Savers candy for candleholders.

The village has been short of meat this winter, but fortunately the situation eased when the hunters killed a few seals last week. We recently donated 100 pounds of dried beans to the Village Council from the school's kitchen pantry. This will be distributed to families to add a little variety to their diets as the people have had little or no meat and are growing tired of potatoes.

We also have some emergency food in storage for use in case the shortage worsens. However, Savoonga is a long way from such an emergency.

Tod is trying to organize a canning project through the Village Council for next spring. He envisions that a part of each walrus that is taken be given to the village. The meat would be canned in the school kitchen and then stored until the following winter in the event meat becomes scarce again.

We have lots of cans that were sent by the government. In the past, the villagers have canned walrus meat, but instead of storing it for the future, they opened the cans right away and ate the meat.

Walrus is Savoonga's favorite dish. The people won't eat anything else if walrus is available. In the spring, they kill so many walruses that often the meat spoils before they can eat it all. Much of it is fed to the sleddogs. If some of the walruses were canned, the supply of meat would be more evenly distributed throughout the year.

Love, Doris

❖ ❖ ❖

Sunday, March 16, 1952

Dear Glad,

We were delighted to get your letter of February 20. I must respond quickly to catch the mail going out to Gambell.

I'm so glad you liked the carving set. Yes, the mottled part is the inside part of the walrus tusk, just like the inside of our teeth. That was made of new ivory. The carvers also use fossil ivory, which is a deep tan color.

At one time, there was another village, Kukulik, about 10 miles east of Savoonga on the next cape. It was wiped out by a mysterious illness about 50 years ago. Some reports have it that the villagers ate raw meat from a diseased seal that caused immediate death. That hasn't been entirely proven, but the fact remains that the people all were found in exactly the positions they were in when they died, reminiscent of the Roman town wiped out by the eruption of Mount Vesuvius.

Assorted tools and other artifacts were found at the Kukulik village site, and Savoonga villagers still go there to dig for ivory, which has changed color after being buried underground. Several archaeological expeditions visited Kukulik during the 1920s and 1930s.

It is still snowing here. Savoonga has had more snow this winter than any other year in recent memory. And the winds have been more intense than usual.

Tod talks by short-wave radio to the Alaska Communications System (ACS) in Nome each morning and afternoon. ACS is Alaska's version of Western Union. At night, Tod usually talks to the teacher in Gambell and to the ANS in Nome. However, the ANS representative was killed in an airplane crash about two weeks ago, so the Nome calls have been cancelled for the time being.

Well, Tod is busy with his yo-yo again, so I guess it is time for dinner. Will write again soon.

Love, Doris

❖ ❖ ❖

Thursday, March 20, 1952

Dear Ashfords and Grandma,

We may have given a false impression of St. Lawrence Island in our letters.

We should have said that there are only three non-native residents HERE. But there are quite a few non-natives elsewhere on the Island. In Gambell, the other village, there is a school with two outside teachers, a Civil Aeronautics Authority (CAA) station with a few outsiders, and on both ends of the Island there are U.S. defense radar sites with upwards of 30 military personnel on each site.

Since the radar sites are secret, it is just as well that you don't mention them. You can see by looking at a map why St. Lawrence, which is so close to Siberia, is a good site for radar stations.

You were right; there are around 550 native people on the entire island— about 250 here and a little over 300 in Gambell. We rarely see non-native people because the 40- to 50-mile dogsled trip between the villages discourages travel. So, we might as well be the only non-native people on the island, given our isolation. However, we do lots of visiting with the villagers, and often provide beds and meals for visitors to Savoonga.

A funeral for an old woman who died recently was held yesterday in the church. Neither Doris nor I went, as I was about half-sick for some reason or another. As it turned out, I'm glad we didn't go. The missionary reported all the details. The body smelled to high heavens, as no embalming is done here. All the church doors were wide open, but the odor was so bad Alice almost became ill.

Everyone was holding their breath. The funeral had been delayed, the body was bloated, and everyone feared the poor woman's body would explode. But they got through the ceremony and carried her body to the cemetery on a dogsled.

In Savoonga, the bodies are not buried in the winter because the ground is frozen solid, so her body was left in a box on the snow. She will be buried in the spring when the ground thaws.

Well, enough prattle for now. I'll write again before the next mail goes.

Love, as always, Tod

❖ ❖ ❖

Monday, March 24, 1952

Dear Mother,

My, the winter is flying by. The days are growing much longer. The sun is setting at 6:30 p.m. and rising about 7 a.m. We have only about eight more weeks of school. Our school year ends about the middle of May because that is when the walrus-hunting season begins.

Honestly, I will be glad when school ends. We have a lot of work to do around the school this summer, but it will be nice to do it on our own time. We must paint the roof of the building and a section of the exterior where the paint is peeling. It was painted last summer, but part of it must be redone. We want to repaint all the school rooms, too. When the *North Star* comes, we will get the paint we ordered to paint our living quarters.

I don't have much news. All the visitors have left, and we have been alone for some time. We are both well, but I'm getting fat. I exercise all I can, but I will do better when I can get outside this summer.

Alice and I are going to hike into the hills behind the village, which is a good day's outing, and Tod wants me to help with the painting. So, I'll have plenty of time for exercise.

Love, Doris

❖ ❖ ❖

Dear Mother,

Tonight, we are experiencing a windy, stormy night more typical of March than April.

We have only six more weeks of school! I didn't teach on Wednesday. The day before, Grace had given me a second typhoid shot. It laid me low. The first typhoid shot affected Tod the same way. We will have booster shots every year.

I'll try to answer some more of your questions. The villagers earn money by carving ivory and selling it to the store which, in turn, sends it to the ANS arts and crafts section, which wholesales the ivory artwork to other sales outlets. The men trap white fox during the winter. The current price for fox fur is depressed—only about $6 for a prime pelt. Twenty to 30 years ago, the price was $60 for a prime pelt. At present, the men are hired as laborers for a military construction project at the eastern end of the Island.

Savoonga, said to be one of Alaska's wealthiest Eskimo villages, receives numerous mail orders from Sears every month. The main food, of course, is meat hunted on or near the island. However, the people supplement their diets with non-native food they buy from the store.

Most of the families use dishware, as you do. Yes, under their parkas, the villagers dress pretty much as we do. Almost everyone wears blue jeans, which are easy to wash and practical. Almost everyone has a pair of high rubber boots to wear during the summer months when the tundra is marshy.

We cannot garden here. Because the ground is frozen near the surface, the topsoil is too cold for planting. Of course, I wish we could grow fresh vegetables. But we did order apples, oranges, and grapefruit that should come on the *North Star* next summer. Alice also ordered cabbages and bananas, which she is going to divide with us.

You talk about robins and forsythia! All we can see is snow and little else. It won't melt until June.

I am sorry to report Ruth Miklahook no longer works for us. Somehow, she got it into her head that Tim Gologergen was attacking her every time she hung clothes up in the utility room at the back of the school. What an imagination Ruth has! Tim wouldn't have had the opportunity to harm Ruth even if he had the inclination.

I once enjoyed Ruth's gossip but now realize her rumors can be hurtful to others. Everyone in the village takes her with a grain of salt. I have hired a replacement—Ora Gologergen, Tim's sister-in-law.

The bathtub drain is frozen. I'll be happy when it thaws so we can heat water on the stove and take real baths in the tub. Taking a tub bath is one of the biggest pleasures of life up here. I've been washing in a thimbleful of water for so long.

Well, I have just lost an argument as to who is going to mix some Cokes for us. Tod claims that isn't a male activity, so I guess I'll have to do it. He even has me strengthening my stomach muscles by carrying in water from the tank in the utility room. I have gotten so flabby.

When we took a long walk last Saturday, my legs ached so much that I could hardly get home. Tod was shocked. He insists that I take a long walk every day to get back into shape. Alice usually goes with me on weekdays, and Tod goes on weekends.

Well, I must get busy with those Cokes. Will write more later.

Love, Doris and Tod

❖ ❖ ❖

Sunday, April 13, 1952

Dear Mother,

Today is Easter, and I have been thinking of how we spent last Easter together. Remember what a warm, sunny day it was? We went out to Lakewood to see the Easter parade.

Today is much different here. It is windy and cold. We have huge snow drifts that completely cover the lower half of our living-room windows.

Alice was planning to leave tomorrow for Gambell, hoping to catch an Army flight to Fairbanks for an Alaska Presbytery conference next week. The way it looks now, I doubt she will be able to leave.

Last Saturday, the wind blew hard from the south. By Sunday, the ice floe had been blown some distance out and there was a lot of open water. This is good for hunting and especially welcome now because there is no meat in the village. Alice talked with the church elders and decided to postpone church so the hunters could go out.

The men shot several seals, each weighing about 300 pounds. Early Monday, they went out again. By 8 a.m., they had taken two walruses weighing about 3,000 pounds each. Tim's crew took one of them. He sent his sister to teach in his place, so he could go back and hunt the rest of the day. Altogether, the men killed three walruses and about 20 seals. The villagers were giddy with anticipation of this fresh meat supply.

Most of Tod's older boys were helping with the skinboats and didn't come to school at all. The younger boys did not return in the afternoon. Their job was to watch for returning hunters, then take the dogsleds out to the edge of the shore ice to load the meat and bring it back to the village.

It was a great day. Even the dogs got fed, which was a relief. We had been worrying about them. They were getting fed only about once in two weeks. A dog belonging to our closest neighbor had starved to death.

After school, we walked out to the edge of the ice where the men were butchering a seal. One of the captains offered Tod a small piece of seal meat, which he tied up with string for Tod to drag home, native style. The crews thought this was hilarious.

▲ *Never having eaten seal meat, Tod asked for a meager share, much to the amusement of the hunters.*

We soaked the meat overnight in salt water and cooked it with onions in the pressure cooker. I didn't like it. I admit, I have fussy tastes. Although we didn't care for seal, we could live on it, if necessary. We hope to get some walruses this spring. Alice says it tastes like tough beef.

Tim promised to take Tod hunting with them on Saturday. Tod was all ready to go, but when he got up at 3 a.m. the wind was blowing so hard they didn't go. Tod cannot hunt with them, as it is illegal for non-natives to kill walruses and seals. However, he will have a lot of fun and can take some good photos, I hope.

Good-bye for now. I'll be glad to hear from you when the plane comes on Tuesday.

Love, Doris

❖ ❖ ❖

Tuesday, April 22, 1952

Dear Mother,

The little ivory Eskimo figure I have enclosed wishes you a happy Mother's Day. It is similar to the pin that Tod got for his birthday from Janet Kingeekuk. Her brother made it.

Not much news here. The days are getting much longer. We still see a faint afterglow about 10 p.m., and the daylight returns about 2:30 am. The days will keep adding daylight until June 21, the longest day of the year.

Ice Floes

Perspective: Ice floes vital to the success of walrus hunting

EACH SPRING, the Savoonga men hunt walruses to feed their families.

A poor hunting season can have dire consequences. The men wait nervously for "ice floes" to bring the giant flippered mammals, many weighing more than a ton, within striking distance.

Anxiety turns to jubilation as walruses from a successful hunt are butchered on the ice floes, brought to the beach, and the meat distributed throughout the village to those in need.

The ice floes are important. Late in the year, new ice floes form on the surface of the Arctic Ocean and Bering Sea as ice crystals collect into pancake-like layers that thicken and stack up on one another. The growing floes move south with the predominant north wind, cracking the ice and forming large chunks that resemble icebergs.

The most successful walrus-hunting requires open water between the shore ice and the ice floe to give villagers access to the hunting ground at the edge of ice floes.

When ice floes come, the men are ready with their umiak skinboats, heavy harpoons, inflated sealskin floats, and high-powered rifles. The success of the hunts— or lack of it—determines whether and how well their families and others in their clan will eat until the next walrus-hunting season a year or so away.

The walruses spend most of their time underwater. But in between dives to the

▲ ▶ *Above and top right: Walruses rode south into the Bering Sea on ice floes, which were importa*

seafloor, where they feed on invertebrates such as shrimp, clams, soft-shell crabs and sea cucumbers, they occasionally rest on the ice floes. That is where they are killed.

The meat, blubber, skin, and organs are rich, nutritious foods favored by the villagers, while the hides are tanned to cover the frames of boats. Traditional drums for Eskimo dancing are made from the stomach lining. The large ivory tasks are carved into artwork, jewelry, and a variety of handicrafts.

The hunting season is over when the floes melt or recede northward.

nting grounds.

After this week, we will have only three more weeks of school. I look forward to a little change. We will be painting the living quarters and will keep busy, but at least it will be a vacation from the little "monsters."

The most discouraging thing that happened to us has to do with our grocery order for next year. We sent it to a wholesaler in Seattle where the Presbyterian Board of National Missions buys supplies for its Alaska missionaries. The company returned our order saying it did not have sufficient inventory to handle it. We immediately sent the order to the ANS representative in Seattle, but we don't know if it got there in time for our order to make the first trip of the *North Star*. The ship leaves Seattle on May 1 and is due in Savoonga around the first of July. If our order is not on board, our food won't get here until October.

We are enjoying spring weather. We spent most of the afternoon painting the roof. I took some color photos.

Alice will be coming back from Gambell on Monday. She has been there for two weeks. From what we hear, the teachers at Gambell are not going to return next year. I wish we had all their modern conveniences, but I wouldn't want to leave Savoonga for Gambell, as the people here are much nicer.

Tim went to Nome last week to get his teeth fixed and brought back a five-pound beef roast for us. We cut it in half and are saving the other half until Alice returns. We usually share our special treats with her, and she does the same with us. We decided not to invite Grace Crosson. We have had her over for at least 15 meals. So has Alice. And Grace never once has invited us over.

Tod and I believe Grace's failure to invite us to her quarters for a meal may have to do with her having been a missionary nurse for several years, during which time the Episcopal Church paid her only $900 a year. You know how some ministers feel they should be entertained gratis. Alice certainly doesn't feel that way.

Anyway, we decided not to have Grace for dinner again until she invites us over at least once. See how petty we get, living by ourselves for so long?

A couple of days ago, the Kingeekuks gave us a crab that one of their boys caught. Everyone in the village has been getting them. We boiled the legs in salt water and then dipped the meat in melted butter. Yum! It tasted like lobster. I dug out the rest of the meat and last night made southern crab cakes—something like salmon patties. I found the recipe in *Good Housekeeping*.

We have seen Army planes passing overhead on their way to Gambell. I suppose they are delivering supplies to the Army post before the ice melts. Gambell expects at least one more Alaska Airlines plane, due April 29, and possibly a second in April, and a third in May. I do hope so.

Well, I must get busy and dash off another couple of letters.

Love, Doris and Tod

11

Walrus Hunting

*Tod's hunting expedition
was exciting. He went along to help
with the skinboat and take photos.
The crew took two seals and
did battle with a walrus.*

❖ ❖ ❖

Tuesday, May 6, 1952

Dear Mother,

Here it is May already, and the snow is still several feet deep. But the days are getting much longer. The sun came up this morning at 3:03 and set tonight about 9:15. I just took a photo of a beautiful sunset.

The mail just came in, and our living room is a mess. Alice is in the kitchen wrapping a package to send out, and Tod is going through the magazines, while Grace is getting the clinic ready for her departure tomorrow. I want her to take this letter to Gambell so it can get out on the next plane.

Tod went walrus-hunting last weekend and hopes to go again Saturday if the weather is good. A woman in the village is making him a pair of waterproof knee-high sealskin boots for hunting. A lot of spray and water comes up and gets him wet in the skinboat. He will wear his walrus-intestine raincoat over his parka, too.

Tod's hunting expedition was exciting. He went along to help with the skinboat and take photos. The crew took two seals and did battle with a walrus.

The idea is to shoot the walrus so that it is wounded but not killed. Then, when it comes back up for air, the skinboat races over and the hunters harpoon it with a sealskin sack that is inflated to keep the walrus from sinking. But this powerful old bull would not cooperate. He thrashed violently in the sea and even threw itself right out of the water. Then someone shot him again. The bull died but sank before he was harpooned. So, that walrus was lost.

I hope to get a light meter to improve our photography. The Presbyterian Board of National Missions sent Alice five rolls of color film that she will share with us, so we will have film for the year. Alice takes few photos. She has so many already.

We have been eating like kings lately. While in Gambell, Alice wired a friend in Anchorage to send some fresh food on the CAA supply plane. The friend sent ten pounds of hamburger, a frozen frier, fresh tomatoes, cottage cheese, celery, lettuce, and cabbage. Alice even borrowed a movie in Gambell—Kipling's *Soldiers Three*. Quite good.

We expect an ANS doctor to visit the village soon to hold a clinic. He will probably stay with us. More company: an Air Force warrant officer from Gambell is coming over, too. How kind of Alice to invite him to stay with us! The officer promised to bring fresh steaks and a movie. So, we will be doing lots of entertaining.

Well, it is almost 10 p.m. Alice is still here, reading our magazines, while we madly work to get letters answered. Rumor has it that another plane will bring mail to the island on May 20, but I am skeptical. The snow is softening, and I don't imagine airplanes will be able to land much longer. Must close for now.

Love as always, Doris

❖ ❖ ❖

Monday, May 19, 1952

Dear Mother,

We finished school last Friday with a little program that night for the parents. The children sang songs they learned in music this year. Everyone seemed to enjoy it.

During the last two days of school, we cleaned the building thoroughly and put away school supplies. The older students helped, scrubbing the floors, washing the walls and windows, and so forth. You would never see children in the States helping this way!

I have been working on records that must be sent to Juneau. I completed the Annual School Report and the School Census last week. Today I am working on attendance records. Grace is in Gambell, so Tod is out on sick calls today. Last night, one of the girls burned her foot badly with scalding water. The water got into her overshoe and just sat there. Before she could remove her shoe, she had a serious burn. There was not much Tod could do except keep the wound clean and administer pain medicine.

I have washed the kitchen walls and ceiling and hope to begin painting tomorrow. I want to get busy and wash the bathroom, too.

The weather has been terrible here the past few days—foggy and damp. Despite less-than-ideal conditions, I noticed that some crews have gone hunting anyway.

Tod insisted that I not ask any of the men to take me hunting, much as I would like to go, because it would put them on the spot if they didn't wish to take me. The women made a fuss when they heard this (from me) and asked their husbands to take me. Since then, I've received three or four invitations! We will wait for better weather and a good day when the men are getting lots of walruses, so I won't have to be out long.

I am having a summer school of sorts. Six of my first-graders are being promoted into Tim's second-grade class. I want them to learn as much as possible before they go and not to forget during the summer. They come to school each morning to complete some of the first-grade work that was unfinished. I give them a story to read at home each evening and some assignments in their workbooks. They seem to enjoy it. Some day when the sun is out, I want to take their photos.

I am also starting piano lessons at the church next week. I am still practicing myself.

I haven't read much lately except for mostly magazines. I read a condensation of *Mr. President* in *Readers Digest,* and I have been following the Whittaker Chambers articles in the *Saturday Evening Post.* I also read *Lorna Doone* by Richard Blackmore and enjoyed it immensely and have begun *The Fountainhead* by Ayn Rand.

I have no more news and have a couple more letters to write before the mail leaves.

Love Doris

❖ ❖ ❖

Tuesday, May 27, 1952

Dear Mother,

I'll add another note to my letter as we just heard a plane go over Savoonga on its way to Gambell.

We got telegrams yesterday saying that some of the boys and girls who spent the winter at the Mt. Edgecumbe boarding school are on their way home. We believe that Alaska Airlines may fly them right over as there are five young people from Gambell and one from Savoonga, Tim's brother. The snow is getting so soft that soon it will be impossible for planes to land on Lake Troutman in Gambell until the ice melts, at which time an amphibious plane will be put into service during the summer.

The Annual Spring Hunts Fed the Village for an Entire Year

TOD WAS INVITED on a hunt in May 1952. Being a non-native, he was not permitted to engage directly in hunting walrus, but he helped with one of the skinboats, took lots of photos, and was thrilled by the experience.

▶ Clarence Pungowiyi scanned the icy horizon. ▶ ▶ Far right: Top, a dog team dragged the hunters' skinboat to the water. Middle, hunters maneuvered a skinboat through a jumble of ice, and bottom, tension mounted when a walrus herd was sighted.

Far left, top, the typical bull weighed several thousand pounds. Above, the hunters pulled a bull walrus out of the sea. Left, villagers waited for the hunters.

I am making bread with high hopes, using a recipe from the *Better Homes and Gardens* cookbook.

Ora Gologergen will be coming in occasionally to help me with housework this summer. I have more time now and can do most of the work myself. I want to save money this summer. Ora will do the washing, but I will clean up the house and do lots of the odd jobs that she does during the winter.

The floe ice is far out, and some of the skinboats are hoping to be able to go to Gambell this afternoon. They will pick up Abner, Tim's brother, and the nurse, and bring back the mail.

We closed school on May 16 and theoretically are on vacation. In fact, we are working harder than ever. Tod helped me paint the kitchen, and he has been painting some of the school rooms. I want to wash the bathroom this week and get it painted next week. Meanwhile, I am busy with the annual school inventory, which is a big headache.

The last teachers, we hear, were rather backward and couldn't seem to do anything right. I found evidence of their incompetence in the shoddy records from last year, which I need for my reports. So, this work has taken longer than it should have. But the paperwork will be easier next year.

By the way, when you go downtown, please buy a few boxes of little stick-on stars and dots. I will try to bribe my little ones to be good by giving them stars on their foreheads or wrists.

We haven't been hunting yet as the weather has been damp and foggy. But the days are getting so long. There is never any real darkness now, and I suspect that when the sun comes out again we will have sunlight until 10:30 p.m. or so. It is still light when we go to bed, and we're finding it difficult to sleep.

Well, I must get back to work. I want to run over to the post office with these letters that will go out if Joseph Noongwook, the mail carrier, leaves for Gambell with his dogsled team this afternoon.

A medical ship, *Health,* a floating clinic that visits coastal villages, will anchor off Savoonga in a few weeks. I can barely wait to see a dentist as I have a painful cavity.

Oh, good news—our food is coming on the FIRST trip of the *North Star.* After all the trouble and anxiety, Mr. Farrell, the ANS representative in Seattle, was able to get it on the spring sailing. We are looking forward to its arrival around the first of July. We ordered a wider variety of food for next year. We are so bored by the foods we have.

More later.

Love, Doris

P.S. I am now reading Vol. 2 of Winston Churchill's *History of the Second World*

War. I'm enjoying it immensely. Alice receives the volumes as they are published and shares them with me.

❖ ❖ ❖

Tuesday, May 27, 1952

Dear Eunice, H. F., and Boys,

We finished school on May 16. There was no point in going any longer. Most of the men were at Northeast Cape working on the radar project, and all the boys 12 and older had to go out in the skinboats as this is their critically important walrus season.

We heard a cute story on the radio the other night. Seems a fellow was in a Russian labor camp. Each night, the prisoners were frisked thoroughly to be sure they weren't taking anything out with them. This fellow came to the gate each night with a wheelbarrow filled with straw, and every night the guard carefully searched the straw, finding nothing.

The guard, who was curious, stopped the laborer one day. "I'm being transferred to Siberia, and it won't make any difference if you tell me what you've been smuggling out for the past six months. I promise I won't tell a soul. What are you smuggling?"

"Wheelbarrows!" said the laborer. Honestly, that is the *only* joke we've heard all winter. So, if you've heard any good ones, or bad ones for that matter, please pass them on.

Well, I must get this note over to the post office. Will write soon.

Love, Doris and Tod

❖ ❖ ❖

May 27, 1952

Dear Eunice, H. F., and Boys,

I have reached the same state I was in while in the Army in Japan—boredom, boredom, and more boredom.

The only topics I must write about are the weather, school news, and the people. I guess that's about all anyone anywhere writes letters about, but the subjects seem less eventful here. I shall continue to write, however, for I like to receive letters. I know that when I stop writing, so does everyone else.

The villagers are cutting and drying their walrus meat, and I have been dressing numerous cuts on their hands. The nurse is in Gambell.

Will you send me your recipe for raised doughnuts? I have tried making them from a recipe I found in the *Good Housekeeping Cookbook*, but they did not turn out well. Our yeast is stale. That may have been the problem. They were heavy as lead, but the flavor was good. We gave them away, but I want to try again with your recipe.

I have a new hobby—fancy cooking! I've added pies and cakes to my repertoire that includes raised doughnuts. Doris discourages my culinary artistry because I tend to make a mess in the kitchen.

I may have told you I went walrus hunting with some of the men. I had hoped to go again soon, but the weather has been poor. Last Saturday, three skinboats got caught on the floe ice and were carried some 20 miles down the coast. It took the crews until 5 a.m. to get back to the village. I'm glad I missed that little excursion.

I have been doing lots of reading. Tell H.F. he can find *Taps for Private Tussey* by Jesse Stuart in the 25-cent pocket-book edition. He will enjoy it no end. The first 50 pages aren't too hot, but you will eat up the last part of it. It's one of the best books I've read in some time. I may have enjoyed it because the characters remind me of my Okie relatives, but it is certainly well-written.

I'm staggering through two volumes of Doris's college history textbook. It seems I got all the way through high school and college without ever taking a course in American history. Then I up-and marry a history major and my life gets complicated. Not that I'm being brow-beaten. But since I have the time, I guess I should pick up a basic knowledge of our country's history. Write often.

Love always, Tod

P.S. from Doris. His protest about being bored does NOT mean that Charles Ray is bored with his wife, Doris! We seem to be getting along well. By the way, we have set up a ping-pong table, and I'm getting so I can beat Tod occasionally.

❖ ❖ ❖

Tuesday, June 3, 1952

Dear Mother,

Our mail service has been steady lately. There were two deliveries to Savoonga in May, and we hear Alaska Airlines may try to get into Gambell once more in June.

We received our mail Saturday night, including the box of candy you sent for Tod's birthday. What a treat! By Sunday, the candy was completely gone. Need I say we enjoyed it? I have been making fudge lately. It gives us so much pleasure!

We are making plans to travel Outside next summer, having decided to return to Savoonga for one more year. We are eager to take to the road to see family around the country. We may ask you to price new Fords and Chevrolets for us. We spend half our time reading reports of new cars in *Popular Mechanics* and looking over automotive advertising. Tod seems partial to the Fords. We think we want an emerald-green model. They are so pretty.

The teachers in Gambell are leaving this summer. We hope that friends in Boulder, Colorado, will apply for those jobs. We could visit them occasionally and help them with any problems that arise.

The Nome ANS administrative assistant who died last winter will be replaced by Lawrence B. Williams, principal of the school at Barrow.[8] Previously, Mr. Williams taught seven years in Savoonga. We are gratified, as he will be familiar with the villagers and understand our problems from first-hand experience. The villagers hope he will visit soon.

Our shore ice is breaking up fast as the weather improves. The territorial medical ship, *Health*, should be here in a couple of weeks. I am anxious for it to come as I have a bad cavity in one of my teeth. Then, the *North Star* will arrive about July 2. We are eagerly awaiting our replenished and more varied food supply.

While in Gambell, Alice traded one of the frozen chickens she had flown in from Anchorage for a canned whole chicken. We are anticipating a chicken dinner next Saturday. Evidently, I have been designated to cook it. Grace returned from Gambell yesterday with a canned Hormel ham. So, we will be eating well even before the *North Star* arrives.

Tod just howled when he read your advice to me to rest and relax. He says I relax sitting down about 20 hours a day and if I were any more relaxed, I'd be dead. Be that as it may, I have gotten much accomplished since school ended. There has been plenty to do.

Well, it is almost time for lunch. Will write more later.

Love, Doris

P.S. You wrote that you were reading *Hearth in the Snow* by Laura Buchan. Buchan is the maiden name of Laura E. Jones, who wrote you from Juneau last fall. She is our ANS supervisor. We haven't read her book yet.

❖ ❖ ❖

---

8. Barrow no longer exists by that name. In 2016, residents of Alaska's farthest north town, previously known as Barrow, voted to rename the city to the traditional Inupiaq name of Utqiagvik.

Dear Eunice, H. F., and Boys,

Tod and I spend so much more time together than most married couples. There are only a few hours a day that we are apart, and even then, we keep tabs on one another from our respective classrooms. It is amazing that we haven't had any serious fights given that we see so much of each other in a place so isolated that we can't get away from one another. (Editorial comment from T.R.: "Horse manure!")

The shore ice is almost gone. We had a high wind for several days last week that broke up the ice. It won't be long before the ships come in.

We are trying to get all our letters answered today, as some skinboats may try to get to Gambell as soon as the slushy ice moves out a little. The shore ice that broke off is drifting around near shore, making navigation difficult.

Our mail service has been unusually reliable the past month. We received two deliveries in May, both unexpected, and Alaska Airlines hopes to make one more flight into Gambell in June. Then the *North Star* may bring mail, and a Coast Guard cutter coming in August may have mail for the village also. So, we aren't nearly as isolated as we were last fall. Write soon.

Love, Doris

❖ ❖ ❖

Dear Eunice, H. F. and Boys,

Although school is out, we have been busier than ever painting, cleaning up, and dealing with paperwork. It is nice to get away from the kids for a spell, but we will be ready to start school early next fall.

I may have told you that we received another raise that increased my annual salary to well over $5,000 and Doris's to more than $4,000. This works well for us financially because our expenses are so low.

The big item that has sold us on this area is the excellent attitude of the people. They treat us like their own family, and we are mentioned often in their prayer groups, asking that we be protected and cared for.

There are screwups here, as there are everywhere, but for every person we dislike there are 10 we are fond of. Isn't that a good batting average?

Last winter, when I picked up a slight cold, a sweet little man who is prominent in the village stopped Doris and told her the reason I had a cold was that I sometimes walk around outdoors without my parka hood closed tightly around my head. He went on to say that she must insist that I close the hood.

The people have offered us enough meat to feed an army. We tried the seal, but it was a bit strong for our tastes. Walrus liver isn't bad, but Doris doesn't like liver of any kind, and I hate to eat a batch all by myself. We have been given locally caught crabs, which are delicious. They taste like lobster. One woman gave us a piece of pork that her husband obtained from the Army at the northeast end of the island. We discovered it had cost him a dollar a pound, but he wouldn't let us pay him for it.

I must tell you about a joke that was played on me. After the mail came last night, we were absorbed reading our letters. The missionary, who frequently makes a pest of herself, bounced down for a visit. We didn't want to be rude, but we were intent on reading our mail. So Doris and I took turns pointedly discussing among ourselves whatever letter one of us happened to be reading. Alice followed right along. Because we had spent so much time with Alice, she knew everyone in our families.

Anyway, I was reading a letter from my friend John Carroll, a law student in Denver. I was paraphrasing like crazy to eliminate John's vulgar language but did not pause to consider the overall inferences. In short, the little quip I read aloud to the Presbyterian missionary was as follows: A fellow in law school asked John if he believed in capital punishment for women. "Naturally," John replied. Where upon the fellow replied, "Oh, then you think women should be *hung* just like men?"

The full realization of what I had read hit me when I finished the last word—too late to back up. Alice stared stonily at the wall, and I giggled like an idiot. In truth, the missionary is not too holy-holy, but I have no doubt that she was shocked.

Write when you have time.

Love as always, Tod

The big item that has sold us on this area is the excellent attitude of the people. They treat us like their own family...

▲ *Tod flew high into the air in the traditional blanket toss.*

12

Ships and Visitors

I think I'm becoming anti-social.
I hate the parade of visitors upsetting
our monotonous routine of doing nothing.
It's assumed visiting non-natives will
stay with the schoolteachers.

❖ ❖ ❖

Thursday, June 19, 1952

Dear Mother,

Summer is flying by. Just two more days until the longest day of the year. Lately we've had daylight around the clock. We have seen some beautiful sunsets and sunrises as the sun dips down just to the horizon, then climbs back into the sky. I look forward to seeing our photos.

After the medical ship *Health* arrived yesterday, the dentist set up a clinic in the school. Thank goodness! He pulled the tooth that had been bothering me all winter.

Today, a thick fog hangs over Savoonga. No one has come ashore, and our skinboats can't go out to the ship. However, we just received word the dentist and his wife, who is also his assistant, expect to come ashore later in the day. They plan to stay overnight, so I'll have to get something ready for supper.

I think I'm becoming anti-social. I hate the parade of visitors upsetting our monotonous routine of doing nothing. It's assumed visiting non-natives will stay with the schoolteachers.

I must tell you about the thrill of our lifetimes. One night last week, Amos Penayah came running over about 11:30 to tell us a walrus was sitting on a big chunk of ice just 100 feet out from the school. Tim's skinboat was already on its way, so we were able to watch the hunt from our front yard, so to speak.

After killing the walrus, Tim and his crew pulled it up onto shore and cut it up. It was a young bull about the size of a heifer. But it was sickly looking and lacked the thick layers of fat that it should have had this time of year. So, the meat was left for the dogs.

Love, Doris

P.S. I'm enclosing a bit of eiderdown one of the women gave us. These down feathers from eider ducks are prized for their use in bedding. Isn't it soft and light?

❖ ❖ ❖

Sunday, June 22, 1952

Dearest Eunice, H. F., and Boys,

We are living in a madhouse!

The *Health* has been anchored offshore since Wednesday. However, because it has been rocking wildly due to rough seas, the ship's doctor and her nurse decided it would be unwise for villagers to come out to the ship. Instead, the two women have come ashore and set up a clinic in the school. They are staying with Alice.

Jack Hittson, the dentist, and his wife Lee have been with us since Wednesday. They are a personable young couple whose company we have enjoyed. Unfortunately, I came down with an infection in my jaw where the dentist injected Novocaine before extracting one of my teeth. My jaw swelled and I was feeling intense pain. Quite worried, Jack ordered me to stay in bed for a couple of days. Lee pitched right in and did the cooking, with help in the kitchen from Tod. Today, I am up and feeling much better again.

Tod and I went out to the ship to have x-rays taken. We both became horribly seasick. And the ship was only about 200 yards offshore! We felt like pikers but were relieved that we both got sick to about the same degree. Our x-rays were negative. Jack and Lee brought in a mess of sea trout they caught along the Alaska Peninsula and froze in a food locker. They also brought in fresh eggs, oranges, apples, and a rib roast.

All our excitement seems to come at once. We expect the *North Star* to arrive next week. In addition, one of the Civil Aeronautics Authority workers based in Gambell was returning there via the Northeast Cape Wednesday night and stopped over here. We could not take him in because all our beds were filled. A medical technician from the *Health*, a nice fellow named Marshall Gordon, was sleeping on a single bed in the spare bedroom. Jack and Lee Hittson were on the hide-a-bed in the living room.

I'm so sleepy I must take another nap. We were given seasick tablets, Dramamine, on the ship. That's why we're both drowsy. Write soon.

Love, Doris

P.S. We had a mess of trout for dinner—the first I've ever cooked. Tod said they were just like his mother used to make them.

❖ ❖ ❖

Thursday, June 26, 1952

Dear Mother,

Just a note as the dentist and his wife may go to Anchorage tonight, and I want them to take this letter with them. The *Health* has been here for the past week. We've all been busy.

Alice and I have spent half our time cooking and half washing dishes. I'll be glad when the guests are gone, and we can settle down into a summer routine again. We expect the *Health* to leave tomorrow night and the *North Star* to arrive Sunday, so we won't have much time to relax.

We hear the new Presbyterian missionary for Gambell and his wife will be on the *North Star*, so I suppose they will come ashore. It will be about two weeks before things get back to normal.

This morning I did a huge wash. Tod carried the water up from the creek. Our tank is nearly empty. Tod wants to fill it today. He will get some help from a few boys in the village.

We had a cheese omelet and cold meatloaf for lunch—delicious food and visiting with friends. This meal reminded us of being in the States. Lee Hittsen brought me some old issues of the *Ladies Home Journal* from the ship. Thanks to her, I will have a satisfying backlog of reading material.

I have piles of dishes, so had better close. I'll write when I can.

Love, Doris

❖ ❖ ❖

Sunday, July 8, 1952

Dear Mother,

The Savoonga villagers put on an impressive celebration for the Fourth of July. It began at 10 a.m. with drills by the local Alaska National Guard unit. Most of the rest of the day was taken up with games and races for everyone, especially the children. A skinboat race was run in the afternoon.

The traditional blanket toss [9] took place after dinner. It was a sight to see! One of the men was propelled into the air from the surface of a walrus skin blanket held up by a group of men around the edges. The men pulled the blanket tight to send someone into the air, then loosened the blanket for jumpers to get their footing before the blanket was pulled tight again. It seems to be a feat to stay upright.

The men wanted Tod to take his turn. So, he did, and I think I got a good photo of him in midair. I hope so.

The *North Star* arrived last Saturday and stayed until Sunday afternoon. The nurse on board invited me out to the ship for a turkey dinner. What a rare treat! I was sorry Tod couldn't come. Someone from the ship was repairing our generators, and Tod had to stay with him.

However, we both were invited to lunch Sunday with Captain Selenjus, a crusty old Scandinavian. The captain expressed wonder about our being together as two of only three non-natives in such an isolated place and asked how long we'd been married. I breezily responded, "Oh, we've been married for 10 months!"

"Vell," he said, sucking on his pipe as he bid us farewell, "You'll either be married for life—or come out in separate skinboats!"

The *North Star* began unloading about 4 p.m. Saturday and worked straight through until the following afternoon. After finishing, some fellows from the ship came ashore to set up a new oil tank at the school. They worked straight through the night, pausing about midnight for a big meal that I cooked. It was no trouble, especially so as they brought food from the ship, including lots of eggs. We still have some of them.

We have been thrilled to eat different things for a change. We have a case of La Choy chicken chop suey as well as beef chop suey. Both are delicious. We put in the pantry lots of chili con carne, tamales, and spaghetti sauce. We have five cases of canned whole chickens as well as a case of boned chicken for salads. Our larder is filled to bursting, and that is the way we like to have it. We also have two

---

9. Traditionally, the blanket toss, before it became a mainstay of native festivals across the North, was intended to give hunters a better look into the distance across a flat terrain or seascape. Some jumpers are said to reach a height of 20 feet.

Everyone Came out to Celebrate July 4th

◀ Velma Pungowiyi came down the wrong way.

▼ Villagers bobbed for apples amid much laughter.

▼▼ The holiday began with close-order drills by the Alaska National Guard unit.

crates of potatoes and one crate each of onions, oranges, apples, and grapefruit. The fresh fruit is refreshing!

Alice's fresh-food order didn't come on the *North Star*. It will come in the fall. So, for now, we are sharing our fresh food with her, and she will do the same after October. This arrangement will stretch our supply of fresh foods.

Our summer weather has ranged from cool to mild. Today it is about 55°, bright, and sunny. Yesterday was foggy and damp, barely above freezing. But the days are still long.

Between visitors, we have been working to get our rooms washed and ready for painting. We finished the spare bedroom yesterday and want to begin in the living room tomorrow. This work had awaited delivery of paint from the *North Star*, and we are determined to get this work finished before school starts.

A territorial sanitarian is expected to arrive from Gambell on Tuesday. He will stay with us until the *Health* returns to pick him up. So, I must get the house cleaned. It is filthy!

Our vacation is half over. We plan to begin school on August 18 so that we can finish by the end of April next year. April is about the time walrus season starts. When it begins, it will be impossible to get anything done as many children are needed to help with hunting and food-processing activities.

We are to be given BCG[10] shots for TB when the *Health* returns. At least I am. Tod's TB test was positive, which means his body already has antibodies to fight TB germs. Alice and I both have negative results, which is rather amazing since we have come into so much contact with TB up here. Anyway, we will be given the serum, which will put the necessary antibodies in our bodies.

Well, the dishes are stacked to the ceiling in the kitchen. I'd better stop rambling and get to work. We are trying to get our mail caught up because the *Health* may take our letters to Nome when it stops here again.

Love, Doris

❖ ❖ ❖

Thursday, July 17, 1952

Dear John and Jim,

We received your nice letters yesterday and appreciated them so much.

I even read them to the missionary, as her mother and father are dead, and her brothers and sisters rarely if ever remember to write to her. Yesterday, when Tod and I received a sizeable assortment of mail, Alice's mail consisted of a single

---

10. Bacillus Calmette-Guerin is a vaccine for Tuberculosis (TB).

letter from her sister. So, we shared some of our letters with her. She enjoyed your letters, too! We all liked the jokes, so if you hear any more, please share them with us.

By the time we get back to the States, you will be accomplished swimmers. Let's have a swimming party when we visit.

Uncle Tod has thought once or twice about jumping into the Bering Sea, but he was discouraged by a few chunks of floating ice left over from last winter. I am going into the water on some bright sunny day so I can boast that I waded in the Bering Sea. But I don't imagine I'll ever summon the courage to go in for a swim. Brrrr!

Do you still have a pet squirrel? The village nurse got a little white husky puppy when she was in Savoonga and then took it to Gambell with her for the summer. He was a fat little butterball and cute as a button. But she told us on the short-wave radio the other day that he had contracted hydatid, a form of tapeworm most dogs on the Island have. It causes a possibly fatal disease if passed on to humans.

We had promised to take care of "Savvy" (short for Savoonga) next winter when she goes to Gambell for another six-month rotation between the two villages. However, we have second thoughts—we don't want to risk catching the disease. We hope she will give the dog back to one of the village families so they can add him to their dogsled team.

One of our neighbors has promised to take us fishing. Likely we will be out on the water all night, fishing with nets. We must dress for the night-time temperatures, which commonly drop to below freezing, even in July.

On Tuesday, the *Health* returned to Savoonga on its way to Gambell. It had been in Gambell for a few days earlier in the summer but developed generator trouble and had to return to Nome for repairs. While there, the ship's doctor bought some fresh food to bring to us.

The ship also brought mail, so we had a real haul. We have frozen chicken, hamburger, fresh tomatoes, cabbage, bananas, apricots, celery, oranges, and lemons. We have been lucky having had so much fresh food this year.

We finally got our living room redecorated. We did it in light green with the ceiling in white. We had ordered the new rubber-based paint from the government catalog. It looks like velvet! We finished getting the room back in order on Sunday and now we are taking a week's rest before starting the bedrooms. Uncle Tod just finished installing a new stove in the living room.

It is getting late, so must stop and go to bed. Write again soon, as we enjoyed your letters so.

Love, Aunt Doris

❖ ❖ ❖

Dear Eunice, H.F., and Boys,

I'll be glad when school starts, so we can get some rest from all this strenuous work!

Our living room was all torn up with the stove moved, rugs taken out, furniture pushed out into the hall, and so on as we repainted our entire quarters. We were in a hurry to get things back in shape, so we washed walls and painted until about midnight for three or four nights in a row. Finally, on Sunday, we moved back in, and since then I haven't felt much ambition.

The teachers before us were a mess in general, but more specifically they had smeared these walls with a couple of coats of dirty kalsomine. We were in such a rush last fall to get school started that we added injury to insult, tacking on yet another coat of kalsomine to avoid having to take the time to wash off their mess.

Finally, this spring, we faced reality and washed off about three coats of the junk from the walls before repainting.

Usually, I don't get too worked up over interior decorations, but now we have the prettiest interior paint I have ever seen. It is rubber-based, soft, and can be washed and painted over.

We've become increasingly fond of Savoonga. The villagers are exceedingly kind and generous. Recently a little girl came to the door, wanting to know if we liked fish. When we said we did, we were graced with a salmon trout weighing several pounds. Two days later, we were given a chunk of freshly caught halibut.

▲ *Everyone shared a halibut harpooned by Elmer Wongittilin and Joseph Noongwook. Delicious!*

We were presented with two murre eggs, too. They are blue with brown specks, and quite a bit larger than a hen's egg. The whites looked like clear plastic when fried, and when I broke the yolk, it was a crimson red. I tried a bite but couldn't get past that red yolk. Doris didn't even try.

We laughed at all the jokes. Sorry to hear about your hand, Jim, but maybe it will heal to such a degree that you can write us another letter before long.

Write soon and often.

Love as always, Tod

❖ ❖ ❖

Dear Mother,

Just a short note as I think a skinboat may go to Gambell today. Not much has happened since last I wrote.

The *Health* returned last Monday. It spent the evening and until 2 a.m. the next day blood-typing everyone in the village. I have Type A. Tod has Type O, which means he can give blood to anyone.

We spent the rest of the week painting. Our bedroom is a beautiful azure blue. This morning, I ironed and hung the bedroom curtains. Our house looks so nice and clean and new. Tod likens it to a honeymoon cottage!

I hate to keep asking for favors. However, I would be so grateful if you would look in the store for Amazo pudding. It is a vanilla dessert, something like Royal or Jello puddings except it doesn't have to be cooked. It is the best vanilla pudding I have ever tasted. You just mix it with milk. I discovered Amazo when Alice received a box. We all loved it! So, if you can find it, I would appreciate having several boxes. They are light and won't cost much to mail.

We just had an accident. Tod was polishing the top of the stove, and a jar of bacon fat fell off a shelf over the stove and spilled all over him, the stove, and the floor. We just finished cleaning the floor, and the grease is burning off the stove.

We received the yellow cloth material you sent. So pretty! I like it. I'll have it made into a snowshirt this fall. Every Eskimo woman and girl must have a new snowshirt to wear for Christmas and Easter. Mae Kingeekuk was sorry that I didn't have a new one last Easter and wanted to make me one from some material she had.

Must close. Time for lunch.

Love, Doris

P.S. August 3. You won't believe what happened in the middle of the night a couple of days ago. At about 1 a.m., I was awakened by a loud knock on our living-room door. I poked Tod. "Someone's at the door."

"Well, go see what they want," he mumbled.

So, I went to the door, and there was a white man, a stranger. I quickly closed the door and rushed back to the bedroom.

"There's a strange white man out in the hall!" I exclaimed.

"Well, ask him in," Tod replied, turning over and going back to sleep.

So, I returned to the door and invited the stranger to come in. He was cold and wet, having come in one of the skinboats returning to Gambell from the radar station at Northeast Cape.

The stranger's name is Henry Michael, an archeologist from the University of Pennsylvania. He has been studying archeological sites. The Gambell skinboat crew had stopped in Savoonga for rest and something to eat with relatives and suggested Henry might get fed at the school.

While I visited with him, I cooked a breakfast of bacon and eggs, which he wolfed down with enthusiasm. Then I made up the hide-a-bed in the living room for him to rest on until the skinboat was ready to resume the sea journey to Gambell.

A couple of hours later, the skinboat captain appeared at the door. It was time to go. I gave Henry a pair of Tod's socks and a sweater to keep him warm. And away he went. It was quite an unexpected adventure in the middle of the night. TOD SLEPT THROUGH THE WHOLE THING!

"There's a strange white man out in the hall!" I exclaimed.

"Well, ask him in," Tod replied, turning over and going back to sleep.

13

Gambell Getaway

*It turned out to be a
miserable, stormy day.
By evening, the weather was
so bad the ship departed.
There we were, stuck
in Gambell again.*

❖ ❖ ❖

Friday, August 8, 1952

Dear Mother,

Today is my birthday, and already I have done a big wash and now am trying to get letters written to send to Gambell tomorrow.

Alice is having a party for me tonight. She gave me an attractive pair of summer boots a few weeks ago—an early gift—so I could wear them during the good weather. Grace had a lovely white sealskin ball with trimmed embroidery made for me in Gambell. Tod is going to have an ivory bracelet made for me on Little Diomede Island. However, he hasn't talked with the teacher up there yet, so it may be a while before I see it.

We have had another busy week. Last Thursday, the new teachers from Gambell, Paul and Mildred Tovey, came to spend a few days with us. Before they were here a day, we discovered that we have little in common with them. Alice shared our opinion. Paul is a smart aleck and show-off while Mildred is reserved to the point of seeming cold and unfriendly.

At any rate, we tolerated them until Saturday night when we were surprised by a visit from the Coast Guard cutter *Storis*. The ship's doctor came ashore to do some medical work while Alice, the Toveys, and I went out to the ship. The captain offered to take the teachers back to Gambell. Since the ship would be coming back past Savoonga the following night, the captain offered to take Tod and me over for the day. We accepted the invitation. An adventure!

▲ *We enjoyed an exhilarating skinboat ride back to Savoonga after visiting Gambell.*
Anthropologist Henry Michael, a visitor to the island, sat behind me.

The ship left Savoonga about midnight and dropped anchor off Gambell about 6 a.m. The captain told us he was running the *Storis* on a single engine so we wouldn't arrive in the middle of the night. Tod and I shared the admiral's cabin. The admiral was not aboard.

However, it turned out to be a miserable, stormy day. By evening, the weather was so bad the ship sailed away. And there we were, stuck in Gambell again, in the middle of the most severe storm we'd seen since arriving on St. Lawrence Island.

In the meantime, for some reason, Paul Tovey had been excessively rude to Grace Crosson, who had been in Gambell for about a month on the start of a regular nursing rotation. She was on the verge of tears.

I'm not sure what this was about. But I felt so sorry for her. I wanted to bundle her up and bring her right back to Savoonga. Grace annoys us at times, but she is so affectionate. She spent most of the day hugging me at every opportunity.

Paul and Mildred Tovey were unpleasant to Tod and me as well, so we had dinner with Grace and her supervisor, Jo Hawes, who was visiting. We spent the night with Mick and Betty Campbell, the new missionaries, who are a little older than we are. They are such a nice couple. Mick just got out of the seminary, and this is his first church. Betty was a nurse before they were married about two months before we were. They made us feel welcome, and we had a nice time, despite the intense weather.

On Monday evening, we watched two movies—*Here Comes the Groom* with Bing Crosby and *Dear Brat* with a second-rate cast. The latter wasn't nearly as good as the former.

When the weather finally cleared on Wednesday, a boatload of us came back to Savoonga. Grace and Jo Hawes came for a few days so Jo could see Grace's work here. Mick

▲ *Lowell "Mick" and Betty Campbell, the Presbyterian missionaries in Gambell.*

Campbell came for a communion service. And Henry Michael, the archaeologist who had stopped in for breakfast in the middle of the night, came to do some work at Kukulik[11], an archeological site near Savoonga.

Mick and Henry stayed with us, but Mick returned to Gambell yesterday soon after the church service. Everyone came to our quarters for dinner last night, and Alice is having us all up to her place tonight.

By the way, the ivory carvings I sent you were not geese. They were swans. There are a few swans on the Island, though I haven't seen any yet. On our way back from Gambell we passed the bird cliffs, summer nesting home of murres, puffins, and auklets. The sky was filled with birds that also covered the cliffs.

These days the temperature hovers between 35° and 50° most of the time, occasionally surpassing 60° on an especially warm day. The tundra is bright green and has delicate little wildflowers growing on it. However, it is wet and marshy. On bright days, the sky is intensely blue. I keep the kitchen stove going all the time, although on warm days I also open some windows to keep the rooms from overheating.

When we were in Gambell, we noticed even more than before the differences between the two villages, and we were reminded of how lucky we are to be in Savoonga. When we got home, some of the villagers told us they had missed us, even though we were gone only a few days.

---

11. The remnants of the seaside village are about five miles from Savoonga. Kukulik is believed to have been decimated by famine in 1879 and 1880.

Five planes came in while we were in Gambell. One of them brought our first-class mail. It was such a pleasure to get letters, even if just a few. Lee Hittson, wife of the ship's dentist from the *Health,* sent me a book of instructions for crocheting left-handed. She says I no longer have an excuse for not learning. So, I may give it a try this winter.

The mail also brought paperwork for the first of my correspondence courses from the University of Washington. I am taking a course in Educational Psychology and another in Psychology of Elementary School Subjects. Unfortunately, I cannot get started because the textbooks for both courses are coming by second-class mail. That means they are sitting in Nome. At any rate, when I finish the courses, Alice will give me the final exams with special permission from the university.

After encountering people with whom we could have been stuck, we're happy to have Alice here. She told me she feels the same way about us. Perhaps my earlier comments about Alice were a little harsh. It's nice to have a good friend.

I'll see what I can do about sending a baby walrus for Christmas. Would you be able to keep it in the bathtub? You would have to put lots of ice cubes in the water, as they are accustomed to living on big cakes of ice. We took a photo of a dead baby walrus being brought in on a sled, and Tod annoys me greatly by showing it to people and telling them it is a photo of me.

Well, I must get some other letters written. Write soon and often.

Love, Doris and Tod

P.S. Be sure to see the July issue of *National Geographic* for an article about the *North Star*. There is a photo of a Savoonga boy, Morris Toolie, being examined by a woman doctor. Also, there is a good photo of a skinboat taken at King Island. Our boats are just about the same.

P.P.S. I also received for my birthday a pretty pair of slippers from Janet Kingeekuk and a pair of Indian vases from Ellie Alowa. Her brother, Tim Gologergen, had sent them to her when he was in the U.S. Army in India. Tim's little girl gave me an ivory knife handle and Ora's children gave me a bar of soap.

❖ ❖ ❖

Saturday, August 16, 1952

Dear Mother,

We are ecstatic to be alone again!

Henry Michael, the anthropologist who has been staying with us, has left for Gambell traveling with Alice, Grace, and Grace's supervisor.

We are busy getting ready for school, which starts on Monday. I am eager to get going so we can begin marking off the weeks until next spring. I finished the village census report last week.

Tod's latest adventure has been catching crabs from shore. After Albert Kulowiyi, the school custodian, made him a crab pole, Tod went off crabbing one evening last week. I walked over to see how he was doing after I finished the radio schedule. He had caught six crabs! We sent three over to Alice and Grace in Gambell, gave Albert one, and kept two. The legs are delicious when boiled. Tod plans to go again on the first clear day.

We hear there is mail for us in Gambell. We are waiting for a skinboat to bring it over, but the weather has been rough for travel by water this week.

Write soon.

Love, Doris

P.S. Saturday Night. We were surprised by the arrival of a Gambell skinboat this evening with our first-class mail. Grace sent over some lettuce, tomatoes, radishes, and green peppers that someone had brought in on a plane. What an unexpected treat!

We hope the Coast Guard cutter will come here on its way south from Barrow after a stop in Nome. The postmaster in Nome told someone that a large room there was filled with mail for St. Lawrence Island.

❖ ❖ ❖

Thursday, August 21, 1952

Dear Mother,

I am having a hard time teaching my beginners and first-graders this year. Does this complaint sound familiar? Like last year, I find it especially difficult working with the beginners who don't know a single word of English when they come to school.

Perhaps you can help. If you have any old copies of *The Instructor* or *Grade Teacher* that you aren't using, would you send them? They would give me ideas for activities and teaching methods. I'm going to order the subscriptions, but I won't see the magazines until next July.

An amusing daily occurrence has been the appearance of Tim's little girl, Linda. She is only five and won't start school until next year. Nevertheless, she marched in on the first day of school, brave as anything, and joined the class. For the past few days, she has been showing up in the afternoons. She is such a good girl. I usually allow her to come in and sit by herself and paint in a coloring book.

Some of the men in the village have been making an outdoor playground for the school. They are building it on a cliff overlooking the Bering Sea. This was the driest place around. They built six swings, a teeter-totter, and a jumping board. I am so pleased! This adds a great deal to the school and will give the children a place to play during recess.

By the way, did you take my Christmas phonograph records home with you when you packed up my things in Colorado? If so, could you send up *The Night Before Christmas*, *White Christmas, 12 Days of Christmas*, and *Silent Night* by Nelson Eddy? We have been thinking of ideas for our holiday program. We may have 12 girls sing *The 12 Days of Christmas or* produce a pantomime of *The Night Before Christmas*.

I don't have any news. Will write more later.

Love, Doris & Tod

❖ ❖ ❖

Friday, August 29, 1952

Dear Eunice, H.F., and Boys,

Life goes along here, as usual—slow!

Alice has been in Gambell for about three weeks. She went over intending to stay for two weeks to help the new missionary with Bible school.

The weather has been so rough that she was forced to spend an extra week. But the water is calmer today, and a skinboat left for Gambell this morning. I'll prepare a good dinner for her tonight. Alice said she will bring some steaks and stew meat. We usually grind up the latter as hamburger for spaghetti and meat loaf.

Alice also picked up eight dozen eggs for us at $1.25 a dozen. That's expensive. Last year, we ordered a whole case of 30 dozen eggs, which become so strong we couldn't use all of them. So, it is better to get a few fresher eggs whenever we can. Grace will bring more eggs for us when she returns.

Well, raise a toast! We're officially an old married couple now. We celebrated our first anniversary on Tuesday. I made a cake for the occasion, or, as I should say, *two* cakes. The first was to be a beautiful, orange sunshine cake, but I made the mistake of putting it in the oven during school and then promptly forgetting about it. By recess time, it was nothing but a charred mess, so I had to make another one.

We started school on August 18. My first grade is doing quite well. I've organized some special prep work to get them ready for learning number concepts. I'm getting some number workbooks on the *North Star* in October, and

The New School Playground Was a Big Hit

▲ ▲ ▲ *The playground was built on a high cliff overlooking the Bering Sea.*
▲ ▲ *Now the children had a dry place to play during recess.*
▲ *Two good friends – Nellie Seppilu and Lynn Pungowiyi.*

I want them to be ready to start working in them.

But, as I've said, the little beginners have me completely stymied. They don't speak or understand a word of English. They are spoiled at home, so they burst out in torrents of tears at the slightest provocation. One little girl cried for a half-hour this morning before I finally sent her home. After recess, a little boy took up where she had left off. And the worst part is that I never know what they are crying about.

I have no news at all. Hope we hear from you soon.

Love, Doris

❖ ❖ ❖

Dear Mother,

The *Storis* returned last Friday and stayed all day. It brought loads of mail for us, including letters, packages, magazines, and a cookbook of Tod's favorite recipes that his mother made for me. I have tried the fried pies already, and Tod has given them his approval. We haven't had any second- or third-class mail since last June!

The ship's doctor and dentist were busy. I went out to the cutter to have the dentist repair a tooth that is capped. The cap had broken. The dentist was able to cement it into place. I expect this temporary fix will last until I get to Detroit next summer. I hope so, as I don't look forward to an expensive trip to Nome, especially not in the middle of winter.

Tod sold his fur jacket to a sailor on the *Storis*. He had bought it on the spur-of-the-moment, and it didn't fit well. He wore it all last fall but hasn't had it on much since getting his heavier parka. He was pleased to have sold it for what he paid.

I may have confused you when I wrote that the school in Metlakatla is going territorial. I should have explained that Alaska has two school systems. We work for the Alaska Native Service, which is a branch of the Bureau of Indian Affairs. The BIA schools are for the native population and are found in isolated places where the community is unable to afford a school.

The Territory of Alaska also has a school system in which the schools are also local in character and have elected school boards. The town or city collects taxes to support its own schools. The larger towns and cities all are territorial. As a village or town grows, many of the ANS schools are turned over to the Territory.

Eventually, we're told, all ANS schools will become territorial, but it will be a long time before isolated villages such as Savoonga and Gambell will be able to support a local school.

You misunderstood about the Gambell school. The new teachers in Gambell taught last year in Metlakatla, a community in southeast Alaska near Ketchikan. It had been an ANS school but responsibility for it was turned over to the Territory this year. Almost all the ANS schools on the Alaska Peninsula were also transferred to the Territory this year. It is primarily a difference in administration rather than curriculum, as we generally teach the same subjects as are taught widely in the States.

Laura Jones, the ANS assistant area educationalist, is scheduled to visit us when the *North Star* stops in October. Remember, Mrs. Jones wrote you last fall? We have several small problems to discuss with her. I hope she doesn't spout a lot of educational theory. Her letters always sound as if she is quoting from a textbook.

Well, I'd better stop rambling, as I have several other letters to write and only a little time in which to do it.

Love, Doris

P.S. It won't be long before mail deliveries will become irregular again, as they were last year at this time. Don't worry if letters don't come for a while and then come in bunches.

❖ ❖ ❖

Tuesday, September 16, 1952

Dear Mother,

We received almost two weeks' accumulation of mail last Friday, yet there was not a single letter from either you or Tod's mother. We felt neglected! However, our hurt feelings healed quickly when we opened a box of our favorite candy bars from Norma Hoyt, a friend of Alice's from Anchorage who visited this summer.

I have no news. The most exciting thing we've done in weeks is to play an occasional pinochle card game with Alice. I'll send this letter to Northeast Cape with one of the men who will fly to the mainland from there as soon as the current stretch of beastly weather breaks. It has been stormy for several days, common weather for this time of year.

Love, Doris

P.S. September 21. An Alaska national guardsman, Sergeant Lento, is here for a few days to look over the Savoonga guard. He arrived last night about 11 p.m. and is staying with us, of course. He promised to take mail back to Nome.

Tuesday, September 27, 1952

Dear Mother,

Just an extra note as Sergeant Lento hasn't left yet. He arrived last Saturday, planning to leave the next day. But he is still here, unable to travel due to bad weather. The sergeant is a pleasant chap who reads a lot. We have enjoyed his company. The weather may break tomorrow.

We haven't had mail for about three weeks. We probably won't see any until the *North Star* returns sometime after October 15.

I am reading a fascinating book titled *Fifty Years Below Zero*, the memoir of Charles Brower, a visiting whaler from San Francisco who married a native woman and lived most of his life at Barrow.

Well, I have no more news and no letters to answer. Will write more later, but I doubt any mail will go out until the *North Star* leaves.

Love, Doris

▲ *A silhouette of the school bell against the sunset.*

14

Checking up on Us

The Alaska Native Service
bigwigs came ashore for all
of 90 minutes. We had much
to discuss . . . but there was so
little time. How frustrating!

❖ ❖ ❖

Saturday, October 11, 1952

Dear Mother,

We have cleaned and polished everything in readiness for the arrival of the *North Star,* which should be here tomorrow if it finishes unloading cargo at Little Diomede Island today.

There are some bigwigs aboard from the Alaska Native Service who are coming on a supervisory visit. Of course, we will try to be on our best behavior. Laura Jones is coming, as are Mr. Irby, head of the agency's personnel office, and Mr. Wilson who is in its resources branch. The *North Star* visit will be brief as most of our freight came on its summer trip.

Grace should be coming from Gambell today. I hope she remembers our mail. Mail for Savoonga has been sitting there for more than two weeks, but the weather has been so bad that no one could mush over to get it.

We haven't heard from you or Tod's mother since August when the Coast Guard cutter was here. I expect, however, that there will be letters from either or both of you coming with Grace or on the *North Star*. If not, we'll assume that you are both dead.

I see lots of activity over by the skinboats this morning. It appears the men are going hunting today.

This letter was interrupted by a noisy commotion outside. A cluster of excited villagers were pointing to something on the other side of the creek. It turned out to be a fur seal that had come ashore. When the men killed it, we dashed over for some photos. It was quite large. Fur seals don't often come up this far north. Federal regulations allow fur seals to be killed only on the Pribilof Islands, though we have seen no indication of enforcement. Who would report violators?

Will close for now.

Love, Doris

P.S. Sunday Night. The *North Star* came and left today. I'm bushed! The Alaska Native Service bigwigs came ashore for all of 90 minutes. We had much to discuss, such as how to better organize classes for more productive teaching and ways to coax the beginners to work in a foreign language—English. But there was so little time. How frustrating!

However, the visitors raved about our quarters, and Mrs. Jones was quite helpful. She told us we were good teachers. She said she knew this by looking over our various projects, most of which we have been working on frantically for the past week so we could impress her. She said she was going to write to you about her visit.

Tod's class had made some lovely picture maps of St. Lawrence Island. Mrs. Jones asked if she could take the best one. My first-graders had made a model of the school in the new sandbox.

I think I'm going to order *Fledermaus* for Alice for Christmas. She is making my bread now. I provide Alice with the bread flour, and she makes bread for both of us once a week. Her bread is so much better than mine. By cooperating, we all have fresh bread more often.

We had THREE mail deliveries in two days and finally heard from you. We could hardly believe our good fortune. First, Grace brought the mail that has been in Gambell for two weeks. Second, while Joseph Noongwook, our mail-carrier, was in Gambell, a plane came in with even more mail. Good timing! Third, the *North Star* delivered yet more mail. What a delight it is working through piles of letters!

❖ ❖ ❖

Wednesday, October 22, 1952

Dear Mother,

The pile of packages and magazines that arrived on the *North Star* included our phonograph and records. We have been playing music constantly. What a joy, thank you! I put your Christmas packages away so we will not be tempted to open them.

It won't be long until Christmas. Groan! That means we will be working on the school Christmas program, which I dread.

▲ *Five of my students worked on a scale model of the school.*

It's no fun dreaming up creative ideas and spending a lot of time teaching the children new songs. However, we do have a collection of rhythm instruments—bells, triangles, and tambourines, etc.—that my kids will enjoy "playing." So, we'll have a performance of some sort for the village.

My little children love the stick-on dots and stars. Thank you for sending them. I have been placing stars on their foreheads after inspections each morning. I'm trying to instill in them the idea that they must scrub their faces, hands, necks, ears, and nails every day and comb their hair.

Yesterday, only eight of my 27 children received stars. I guess they all worked overtime last night cleaning themselves up because today all but two of the children earned stars! They are so proud of themselves. I'm hoping the little ones will learn to wash themselves rather than depend on their mothers or older sisters.

Alice took some photos of me reading the children a story. She used flash bulbs. I hope the photos turn out well.

We won't be able to bring the portable typewriter with us in the spring, as we will be traveling by dogsled. It is a rough trip, and the typewriter would be ruined.

The Christmas records haven't arrived yet, but may come in the next mail delivery, whenever that will be. Some of the boys in the village are going out to an Alaska National Guard encampment in Anchorage around the first of November. They are going to go out on a military flight from Northeast Cape and probably will take our outgoing mail with them.

Tod and I have a running argument over when to turn on lights in the morning. He doesn't like to get up and walk down the dark school hall to the utility room to turn on the generator. Poor man! However, without lights, it is too dark for me to get breakfast at 7:30. Neither of us has won the argument yet, but Tod did get up this morning.

Love, Doris

❖ ❖ ❖

JUNEAU
Friday, October 31, 1952

Dear Mrs. Derby:

You may recall I wrote you last year in reply to your letter inquiring about the welfare of your daughter and son-in-law, the Rays, at Savoonga. I visited them yesterday and felt certain you would be pleased to know that they are both well and happy.

I have been traveling on the *North Star* and by airplane for three months visiting our schools. I found Savoonga to be one of the best in both appearance and comfort.

Doris and Tod are highly efficient as teachers, and we are proud to have them in our service. They have a delightful group of people to work with and an attractive home and school.

They spoke of coming to the States next summer. I know how much seeing them would mean to you and them.

Kindest regards to you.

Sincerely yours,

Laura E. Jones

Education Specialist

Alaska Native Service

❖ ❖ ❖

Friday, November 14, 1952

Dear Mother,

Friday at last!

In truth, this week hasn't been too hard as we had a holiday on Armistice Day. No school. Some men are going to Northeast Cape tomorrow, so I'll try to send this note with them. We haven't had mail since October 12, and probably won't have any until Troutman Lake at Gambell freezes hard. Last year, planes didn't land there until December 23. I hope it will be sooner this year.

I'm sitting in the office with Tod while he relays messages for other schools. We often serve this role for certain schools because our radio signal seems to be stronger than theirs. Radio conditions are extremely poor right now, but earlier tonight conditions were good. We picked up a Denver station.

Tim and I are swapping classes. Now I teach reading, spelling, and language to the second and third grades as well as the first grade. Tim is teaching grades one through three arithmetic and English for the beginners. When Mrs. Jones was here, she suggested I teach reading instead of Tim because I better understood the structure and usage of English. Tim, on the other hand, was better able to work with the beginners because he spoke Yupik.

The wind is howling tonight. I guess the snow is here for good.

Love, Doris

❖ ❖ ❖

Monday, December 1, 1952

Dear Mother,

I am a widow tonight.

Tod and Jacob Seppilu, the store manager, went to visit a shuttered research camp today to borrow some gasoline because the store's gasoline supply didn't come on the *North Star*. Tod and Mr. Williams, the new ANS representative in Nome, checked with the U.S. Coast and Geodetic Survey, which had left several hundred gallons of gas at its camp on the island a couple of years ago.

Tod received a telegram confirming the store could have the gasoline, but first the quantity available at the shuttered camp had to be measured.

We thought the two men would come back tonight, but a storm settled in this afternoon, so I guess they'll wait it out at the camp. Tod took Alice's sleeping bag with him.

In the meantime, Tim isn't teaching. He just returned from an Alaska National Guard encampment. Tim is a second lieutenant in charge of the island's guard unit. This week he must go to Northeast Cape Air Force Station to confer with a colonel there about evacuation plans. The military's evacuation plan in case of war has been for all of us to go toward the Northeast Cape. However, when Tim was in Anchorage, he learned the Air Force wanted to evacuate everyone from Northeast Cape toward Savoonga. So, I guess the military is going to have to straighten this out.

Alice scoffs at all this planning, but I think it is good that such preparations have been made. Grace has an evacuation kit of medical supplies packed and ready to go. The Village Countil has made plans for who is to take whom in case the village must evacuate.

The wind is blustering outside. Nome radio just announced that the temperature there is -2° and was down to -6° this evening at 6 p.m. Our current temperature is about 20° above, but this wind makes it feel like -20°. I'd prefer cold and still any day to warm and windy.

I spent most of the afternoon helping Janet Kingeekuk make birthday cakes for Vera Gologergen's first birthday. Vera is Tim's little girl, but the Kingeekuks have adopted her. I thought only one cake would be needed when Janet asked for help. But she brought me cake mix for three cakes—enough for a party.

I guess I'll send this letter down to Northeast Cape with Tim so it may get out faster.

Love, Doris

P.S. We haven't had any mail since October 12.

❖ ❖ ❖

Sunday, December 14, 1952

Dear Mother,

Finally! We got some mail. In fact, two months' accumulation of letters. It got as far as Gambell a couple of weeks ago. Joseph Noongwook mushed over for it last Wednesday. Thursday was a stormy day so he couldn't return right away. But Friday was beautiful. By 6 p.m., we all were on pins and needles, waiting.

I have even been *dreaming* of mail. Alice came down in the evening to play pinochle to pass the time until Joseph arrived. But neither Joseph nor the mail showed up.

Saturday was a miserable, windy day. Although we knew Joseph had left Gambell on Friday, we figured he might have sought refuge from the storm in an empty camp somewhere along the trail.

I was overwhelmed with excitement—and so were most of the dogs in the village, howling into the wind—when Joseph mushed into Savoonga loaded with mail about 4 p.m. Saturday. I rushed over to the post office and stood by, clutching our letters as they were pulled out of the sacks. Our post office does not have mailboxes, so this informal method of collecting your mail is common.

We had a grand time opening our mail, though by late evening we had felt so much excitement that we felt ill. No kidding! Tod had a terrible headache, and I felt upset too. Alice brought down her projector, and we looked at the new color slides we received after submitting our summer photos for processing.

We were delighted to receive a carton of Amazo pudding from Maxine. Other packages await in Gambell as Joseph was able to bring back only about one-fourth of the Savoonga mail. There is to be another plane in on Tuesday, so Joseph is going over again tomorrow. In the meantime, today we are frantically answering letters we received.

Our absentee ballots for last month's election arrived in the mail—too late to be counted. I consoled myself by finding a Mounds candy bar that I am splitting with Tod. It was stored in the bottom dresser drawer in the spare bedroom, which we keep closed and unheated. The candy bar is as hard as ice—and VERY COLD.

As you may have heard, there is a waterfront strike in Seattle. No ships have been sailing for Alaska, so all the packages and magazines that weren't sent air mail have been piling up. The federal government has sent a couple of relief ships to Anchorage, but the mail is a mess. Fortunately, all our letters come air mail, but some of our outgoing Christmas packages may be late. As a matter of fact, we sent most of our packages by air mail, as this class of service is more reliable and not much more expensive. They didn't weigh much.

You asked about the courses I am taking. Tod started one course but is not finishing it. He just hasn't had the time, and the course is somewhat repetitious of the classes he took in Colorado. I am taking courses in education.

Tod has almost decided that Columbia University is where he wants to go for graduate studies. But it is too soon to apply. Columbia accepts applications no sooner than a year in advance, so he will apply next fall. In the meantime, however, we have written to the Columbia housing office asking to be put on the waiting list for an apartment. The university has two-room apartments with kitchenettes and baths. We would hope to be right on campus, if possible.

I will look for a job as a secretary or assistant to a professor. In that way, I could get free tuition for courses I'd like to take in the late afternoon or evening. Tod has about decided to specialize in elementary administration as there is a bigger demand in that field for men than in almost any other educational field.

As you know, women fill most teaching and administrative positions in elementary schools throughout the country. However, with an increased number of veterans earning college degrees, schools are hiring more men as teachers, principals, and administrators.

I hope the *Fledermaus* record we ordered for Alice is in Gambell. Otherwise, we may have to cut a photo of the album cover out of a catalogue to put into a box for her. None of our Christmas boxes have come yet.

We have been busy working on our Christmas program. It is still in rough shape, and the children won't speak loudly enough. Oh, well, the parents will like it, that is the main point. I have been wrapping gifts for the children. I plan to give pearls to the older girls and toy airplanes and cars to the little boys.

Mick Campbell is coming over for the weekend right after Christmas. Our spare bedroom is a mess! I must clean it, though the door has been closed and I'll have to heat it before I can clean. I better get busy.

I hope that if Aunt Glad gets us a slide-projector for Christmas she will not send it up here, as jolting it for 60 miles on a dogsled will probably break it. Alice has one that we can use, and we have another at the school. So, if Glad intends to get a projector for us, please keep it for us until we come back.

We finally got our shore ice last week. It froze overnight. We were amazed as usually it grows a little at a time—at least it did last year. We don't know if the ice floe has come down from the Arctic yet as we see only ice. The floe had reached Little Diomede and King Island a couple of weeks ago, so it should be here by now. Perhaps that is what we see on the horizon.

We're optimistic about getting away next spring by way of the Air Force station at the northeast end of the Island. Tim was told we could stay there awaiting a flight. Mr. Williams at the ANS in Nome said he would confirm details with the commander of Nome Field when the time comes.

This arrangement will be most welcome because we don't want to exit the island through Gambell. If we flew Alaska Airlines, the single, one-way fare from Gambell to Nome would be $107. So, our cost for two, round-trip tickets from Gambell to Nome would be more than $400—to say nothing of the fare for flights from Nome to Seattle and from Seattle to Detroit. So, if we can go to the mainland with the Army for free to reduce our travel expenses, we certainly will.

Grace ordered a turkey through the CAA for Christmas, but the dogsled teams didn't bring it over. Maybe it will come this week. Truthfully, I'd be content with one of our canned whole chickens. Otherwise, I'll have the turkey to cook and I'm not looking forward to it. Christmas dinner will be at our place, as Alice hosted us for Thanksgiving.

Our school program takes place Christmas Eve. We must put it on twice to accommodate everyone in the village. Later that evening, we will have dinner with Alice. Alice's church program is on Christmas, so Grace will help me.

I probably told you that Grace is a trained midwife. A couple of babies are due in a few weeks, and Grace has invited me to witness a delivery. She has given me a lot of valuable information. When Grace isn't here, the native midwives must use ergotrate in tablet form under the mother's tongue to contract the uterus after the birth. Grace said ergotrate is more effective when administered with a syringe and needle. She will show me how the shot is given so I can give it when necessary. Fortunately, I'm becoming adept with a syringe and needle.

I like the new teaching arrangement better, although I'm not sure Tim does. I didn't like trying to teach beginning concepts of arithmetic to the first graders,

▲ *I looked small among huge chunks of shore ice.*

as they have nothing like it in their own culture. They have a considerably different system of counting—not based on the decimal system of 10. The Yupik numbering system has a base of 20.

So, I am teaching reading and language activities to the second and third grades in the morning, while Tim works with the beginners and first grade. Then we switch, and I teach reading and language to the first grade.

However, Tim prefers working with older children. The little ones, especially the beginners, sometimes have emotional problems that Tim may find difficult to handle. Nevertheless, he can communicate with the beginners, who come to school with virtually no knowledge of English and help them begin to learn a new language much better than I can.

Our mail should come every two weeks from now until we leave in the spring, so you can be more confident that we will get your letters. Likewise, you should get mail from us twice a month.

It is a little after 2 p.m. Grace just had lunch with us. It was her second lunch of the day. A few evenings ago, she had dinner with us at 5:15 and then ate again with Alice at 6:30. No wonder Grace is so heavy.

I must sign off. Every dish in the house is dirty, I must plan dinner, and I have letters and letters to write tonight before the mail leaves tomorrow.

Love, Doris

▲ *Mabel Toolie showed us the white leather she made from seal skins.*

15

'Vacation' Adventure

*We lost the dogsled
trail twice. Visibility was so poor
at times we couldn't see our lead dog.
I frostbit my nose and six toes.*

❖ ❖ ❖

Friday, December 26, 1952

Dear family and friends,

Merry Christmas!

Believe it or not, we got THREE mail deliveries before Christmas. What an improvement from last year. We received most of our cards and opened our gifts from the States on Christmas Day.

Two Alaska Airlines planes flew into Gambell with lots of mail, and a CAA plane came in two days before Christmas with first-class mail, including a bunch of holiday cards.

It has been a hectic week. We had school on Monday and Tuesday, although the afternoons were filled with decorating and practicing for the Christmas program. On Wednesday, we were up early and kept busy all day. I spent most of the morning cleaning an immense turkey that Grace Crosson, the ANS nurse, received by mail.

While I was at this task, the villagers were bringing their gifts to the school. As you may recall, the gifts are sorted by family and then distributed to one another other at the end of the Christmas program. There are special piles of gifts for Tod and me, the nurse, and the missionary. Much of my time during the morning was taken up running in to see how the piles were building up.

We had two showings of the program because Tod's classroom is not large enough to hold everyone. The boys had built a stage with a curtain rigged from an old parachute. The first program began at 3 p.m. and was quite successful, if I may say so myself. It was 5 p.m. by the time all the gifts were distributed.

▲ *Tod and I were given a rug made from the skinned hide of a large polar bear.*

We had dinner at Alice's and then returned for the evening performance, which began at 6. It was not as good as the afternoon program, but the villagers seemed to enjoy it, and we were greatly relieved when it was over. Alice and Grace came over to our quarters and we all opened gifts together.

The gifts weren't as lavish as last year, the novelty of new teachers having worn off, but they were equally appreciated. Tod was given a gun scabbard made of sealskin, a pair of sealskin mittens, an ivory letter-opener, a pair of slippers, and a small carved ivory seal from his special friend, Jimmie Toolie.

I received a pair of slippers made by a little wizened old Eskimo woman who spoke no English. I believe she tanned the leather with urine, an old traditional method. The slippers smelled so terrible we soaked them in kerosene and burned them. But I appreciated the gift immensely because the old woman had worked so hard on them.

I also received a beautiful pair of red and white leather *mukluks* with the fur on the inside, made by Mabel Toolie, Jimmie's wife. I received a lovely bird pin made of old ivory and many sealskin pins trimmed with beads made by girls in Tod's class.

We shared some nice gifts, the most unusual of which was a rug made of a polar bear hide. The bear was killed three or four years ago and must have been immense, judging by the size of the head. We also were given two lovely white fox pelts by Tim Gologergen and Albert Kulowiyi.

We received ivory birds, seals, salt-shakers, and a knife, among other things. One interesting carving included several small figures and birds made from old ivory found at Kukulik, the buried village about 10 miles from Savoonga.

In the summer, the villagers go there to dig for buried ivory and relics. Several anthropologists and archaeologists have visited the site, including Henry Michael from the University of Pennsylvania, who stayed with us last summer. Anyway, the little ivory figures are used in a native game similar to jacks, the ancient game of dexterity in which objects are tossed up and caught in various ways.

I spent Christmas Day preparing and roasting the big turkey. It was my first bird. I got up before dawn (about 9 a.m.) to make stuffing by myself under lamplight. Tod arose a couple of hours later, just as I finished in the kitchen, and promptly declared the stuffing was too dry. Grrrr! I believe stuffing is made differently in each region of the country. Alice and Tod both come from Colorado where people prefer their stuffing moist. Grace comes from New York and likes hers just as I made it.

At any rate, Tod poured in more liquid, and of course the stuffing became soggy and was a mess to stuff into the bird. At dinner, Tod wisely pronounced the dressing to be the best he had tasted since we got married—better than Alice's, even—and was as good as his mother's. So, I was pleased in the end—and mollified.

There was a church program in the late afternoon, so we didn't have dinner until about 7 p.m. It was 10 by the time we finished, having rested between each course. I had four old, shriveled apples left, and Alice was able to salvage parts of a few oranges that hadn't spoiled, so we had "fresh" fruit and whipped cream for dessert. By then we were exhausted.

Today brought no rest. We are expecting Mick Campbell, though it is quite stormy, and he may not be able to make the trip. The teacher in Gambell radioed us that Mick was bringing a movie from the Army post, *Music for Millions*, starring June Allyson and Jimmy Durante.

Mick will stay with us, so I was busy cleaning, as was Alice. I want to get this letter finished so Mick can take it with him when he returns to Gambell. There will be another mail plane on January 6.

We finally received the Taku jackets we ordered. They are waterproof and lined with a detachable zip-in layer of woolen insulation. They have detachable hoods, too. We are pleased with them, though I want to have a piece of fur sewn around the hood to protect my face from the awful wind.

We will teach three days next week and then enjoy a four-day weekend. We would have taken a longer break but needed three days to reach the required number of teaching days before we can leave on schedule in the spring.

We are short on news, so will close for now. Write soon.

Love, Tod and Doris

❖ ❖ ❖

Dear Mother

Thanks for all the gifts!

I wore the slip yesterday with my white nylon blouse and black skirt, which thankfully fits me again this year after being too small for so long. The cologne is so fragrant! Tod is pleased with his new wallet. I expect he will write to thank you himself.

Tod arranged for Mabel Toolie make me a pair of *mukluks*, but she made me *two* pairs—one ornamental pair from her and the other a gift from Tod. The *mukluks* she made for Tod to give me are plain with fur on the outside. Those will be my everyday footwear. I will save the other pair for dry weather in the summer and fall, as the red dye will run if I get them wet. She also made me a fancy pair last Christmas because, as she said, "Gregory like you!" Her son Gregory was a beginner in school last year and is now in first grade. I keep last year's *mukluks*, the fancy ones, for Sundays.

Alice gave us an electric popcorn-popper that also serves as a chafing dish. It hasn't come yet, so she wrapped up a photo of the popper from the Sears catalogue. Grace gave us a set of individual sterling salt-and-pepper shakers. We got a big box of food from Burton and Maxine. She had packed some unusual things—several cans of pie filling (cherry, blueberry, and raspberry); a box of pineapple upside-down cake and gingerbread mix; nuts, candy, and little packages of powder that can be made into jelly by adding boiling water and sugar.

Eunice's family sent Tod a lovely set of cufflinks and matching tie-holder and me a pair of colorful Turkish slippers made of red velvet trimmed with gold elastic. They are unique and so attractive. I intend to save them to wear when we go to the States, although I could not resist wearing them all day yesterday. Tod's mother sent me some cologne and him some stick deodorant and cologne in Old Spice, his favorite scent.

I can hardly believe 1952 is almost over. What a year! After next week, we will have only 16 more weeks of school. Time goes by fast when mail comes every two weeks.

Our bank balances are growing nicely. Our balance is over $6,000. We hope to be able to save $15,000[12] in three years here. As you know, we like Savoonga and have decided we want to teach here for another two years. Then, some of our savings would allow Tod to enroll at Columbia University in New York City for post-graduate studies.

---

12. The equivalent of about $170,000 in 2023 dollars, adjusting for inflation.

Did I tell you, we each received a $200-a-year raise last fall? That will help immensely. But, oh, the income tax we pay! Yes, I know, we are fortunate to be doing as well as we are.

We read a newspaper article recently about a teacher who came to the Alaska Native Service after teaching a few years in Guam. She had good things to say about her experience there. Like Alaska, Guam has many native villages. The territory is administered by the U.S. Department of Interior. We have been thinking it might be a worthwhile experience to teach there after Tod finishes at Columbia. I remember an old boyfriend telling me that Guam is more beautiful than Hawaii.

The salaries for teachers in Guam would be approximately the same as those in Alaska. If we taught there, we might be able to travel home by way of the Far East and Europe. Of course, all this is just daydreaming, but we are intrigued by the possibility.

I must close now. It is almost supper time. We are having supper at Alice's, but I still have some housework to do.

Love, Doris

❖ ❖ ❖

Saturday, December 27, 1952

Dear Eunice, H. F., and Boys,

We were happy to hear the baby arrived with no mishaps though we were crossing our fingers for a girl. Anyway, it's nice to know that in a few years, H.F. won't have to hire labor for his contracting business.

The cufflinks you sent will come in handy. In my poverty-stricken college days, I borrowed cufflinks from my wealthier roommates. I do like French-cuff shirts, so now I'll be in a better fix for wearing them.

To establish myself as a true sourdough, I must tell you about my latest harrowing experience. Strictly in the line of duty, I had to travel to a closed camp about 20 miles away by dogsled to inspect some surplus gasoline left by the U.S. Coast and Geodetic Survey a few years ago. The village store is getting this gasoline because its resupply failed to make the last *North Star* sailing. I was asked to report on its quantity and condition.

The night before we were to leave, I was about to roll over and go to sleep when the fellow with the dog team came to the front door to say we were leaving right away, despite the bad weather. It was blowing hard with a fine snow that reduced visibility. The wind and snow were in our faces all the way, and snowdrifts covered the trail in places. Progress was slow. It took us all day to cover the distance.

We spent most of the night uncovering a cache of what turned out to be about 4,000 gallons of gasoline in five-gallon cans. We spent what was left of the night in a trapper's camp and returned to the village the next day.

Just to keep things interesting, the wind had shifted during the night, its intensity increasing, and slammed into our faces all the way back. We lost the dogsled trail twice. Visibility was so poor at times we couldn't see our lead dog.

I frostbit my nose and six toes.

We finally got back to the village about 6 p.m. Unfortunately, I thawed my frozen skin too quickly and got "chilblains," a painful itching of the skin caused by poor circulation when the skin is exposed to freezing cold. My nose peeled but is now normal, though misshapen. My feet still bother me off and on. Looking at the positive side, if I ever write a book, I can dress up my account of this heroic adventure, make it seem more gruesome than it was, and perhaps sell a few extra copies.

Our Christmas was a big one. Some of our newness has worn off, judging from the more modest gifts from the villagers. But I should add that we probably don't deserve anything elaborate. There is a saying in Alaska that the first year you are in a village, it's "nice kitty!" The second year it's "old kitty!" And the third year it's "skat!" Since we plan to skat anyway after our third year, we won't have to worry about over-staying our welcome.

We have made a lot of friends here. But in my opinion, it's bad practice for non-natives to live in these isolated villages for too long. They become cranky, domineering, and poor neighbors who try to manage the community. I'm thinking specifically of a missionary who has been here seven years. She is long past due for a transfer, and the people are fed up with her. There is a chance she will leave when her tour of duty is up in one more year. If she doesn't go, I suspect the people will make life unbearable for her.

These religious people often give me a pain in the butt, anyway. This so-called "saving of souls" is such a broad endeavor that it justifies all sorts of behavior that I consider out-of-line. The missionary pokes around trying to arrange marriages, especially when an offspring is expected, and sticks her beak into many personal affairs in a way that would alienate anyone.

Your television set sounds fine. I look forward to viewing it next summer. I got my first look at a TV a year ago last fall in Seattle but didn't form a favorable impression. I saw *The Lone Ranger* and *Howdy Doody* in a bar, and that was the size of it.

As ever, Tod

◆ ◆ ◆

Sunday, January 4, 1953

Dear Granny,

Today is the last day of vacation from teaching until we leave in May. The school year is a little more than half over. The time has flown by, but I can see the next few months will be a long grind.

The nurse is contemplating remaining in Savoonga for most of the winter. Her living quarters in Gambell are not as livable as they are in Savoonga, which isn't saying much. We sincerely hope she stays. Having her here would relieve me of the medical duties.

There is another reason. We all intensely dislike the teacher in Gambell, who is a rude smart aleck. He makes life miserable for the nurse when she is there. If the nurse stays in Savoonga, then the teacher must make sick calls during the worst part of the winter. Maybe he will transfer or resign. That is our hope!

Our holiday was pleasant, though our rare sleep-in time was disrupted by the short-wave radio schedule every day at 8 a.m. On Little Diomede Island, a mental patient was causing trouble, and the authorities wanted to move her to an institution. For the past week or so, efforts have been made to get a flight out to the island, but each time the weather failed to cooperate. Because the island has a weak radio transmitter, I was called on to act as a relay between Diomede and Nome. I don't begrudge having to do this. I certainly sympathize with the people there, but this cut into our vacation sleep-in time.

This morning, we heard a storm warning promising gale-force winds and blizzard conditions. I plan to carry in some ice to melt in the water tank, fill the refrigerator with kerosene, empty the toilet, and do all my outside chores before the storm hits.

Despite the forecast, we have been fortunate this year. Neither of us remembers the weather being this nice last year. We'll probably pay for it before spring.

Well, I can't think of anything else that Doris probably won't tell you, so I'll close for now.

Love, Tod

16

Caught in the Middle

■

*Being among the few
people able to read and write well,
we've become unwilling welfare
agents. This thankless job is a
pain in the neck!*

❖ ❖ ❖

Wednesday, January 7, 1953

Dear John Charles,

Thanks for your letter and card.

The next time your folks tell you how spoiled you are, you can tell them—and I'll back you up—that you aren't as spoiled as Eskimo kids. We have learned that these children aren't disciplined at all. They run wild. Their parents dote on them and cater to their every whim. Recently we discovered why.

In their culture, Eskimos believe that when a person dies, his soul is reborn in the body of the next person of the same sex born into their clan, which is not quite the same as a family. The new baby receives the same name as the person who died, and everyone believes that the soul of the dead clansman determines every action of the child.

Ordinarily, the people who die are elders much respected for their wisdom and experience. The people believe that it makes no sense to refuse anything to the spirit of the deceased, thus the child does what he pleases.

You can imagine that this custom makes teaching rather tough. I had to shake one little "errant soul" not long ago until his teeth rattled because he wouldn't mind.[13]

---

13. Corporal punishment of school children as a method of modifying misbehavior has been used throughout the world for centuries and continues today in some countries. However, most western nations have banned the practice. In the U.S., Massachusetts banned corporal punishment in public schools in 1972, and most states, including Alaska, followed its lead.

The missionary recalls visiting a home where she saw a little boy about three years old playing with a sharp skinning knife. She naturally took it away from him so he wouldn't cut himself, handing the knife to his mother. When the child began to cry, the woman promptly handed the knife back to him

On a lighter note, I have a joke you might like. An uncle came to visit his brother and family. Because sleeping space was limited, he had to sleep with his nephew. The uncle was weary and immediately crawled into bed. Before he closed his eyes, he noticed the little boy kneeling on the other side of the bed, presumably saying his prayers. Feeling guilty for being so irreligious, the uncle jumped up, knelt on his side of the bed, and feigned a prayer.

The little boy looked up and said, "Boy, is Mom going to be mad at you!" The uncle asked why, and the nephew replied, "Well, the pot is on this side of the bed."

Tell Jim the only way to get letters is to write them, as I've learned. Be good, both of you.

As ever, Uncle Tod

❖ ❖ ❖

Sunday, January 18, 1953

Dear Ashfords and Sons,

Just a note to let you know I'm still kicking. Did the boys get their *mukluks*? Because of the dock workers' strikes, we have worried about delivery of packages that we didn't send via airmail.

Well, our plans have changed again, but don't take what I tell you too seriously. There's a good chance this won't be the last revision before we set sail for the States. My favorite pastime here is to sit down in the evenings and figure financial budgets. I calculate tentative budgets, tentative salary, and estimated savings. Doris says she can always tell when I'm bored. That's when I get out the pay slips, bank book, and a calendar.

Anyway, I figured the tentative cost of our trip Outside next summer. Allowing liberally for unexpected expenses, it came out to several thousand dollars. This came as a shock. The big expense was the transportation out, with $60 spent just getting to the eastern end of the island where we would hope to catch an Army plane.

This is the new plan to reduce expenses. We will not leave here nearly as early as planned. Instead, we'll finish classes and spend a month and a half getting the school in order and generally puttering around. Then, we will depart via the *North Star*. It comes to the Island about July 1 and then takes about two weeks to go straight to Seattle, stopping only at Sitka.

Because ANS regulations have changed this year, we won't get as long a leave as we expected. However, the time off doesn't start until we reach Seattle or Detroit, we're not sure which.

At any rate, the two weeks on the ship would not count as leave, and the passenger fare for government employees is only $3 a day—not even enough to pay for the good meals served aboard ship. So, we both can get all the way to Seattle for about $100, which is much less than the cost of flying.

Pappy, on another matter: I still haven't found Doris broad-minded enough to allow me to accept the Eskimo hospitality of sharing a man's wife[14] with me when I visit. Will you talk with her next summer and make her see the sense of such an arrangement? I've used all the old adages such as "When in Rome . . ." but to no avail. Ha, ha, joke!

The temperature here has stood at a cool -10° for about a week. That isn't impressively cold but add in a strong wind that pushes the freezing air through the cracks and crannies of your quarters and you have a different story. We are never bothered by the cold when the wind doesn't blow, but with high winds there's just no keeping warm. The cold is going to find you!

Enough rambling for now. Write when the urge strikes you.

As ever, Tod

❖ ❖ ❖

Sunday, January 18, 1953

Dear Mother,

Today is a lovely day. The temperature is -8°, but the sky is clear and the air crisp—a good day for a walk.

It seems like such a long time since I've written. I must relate an incident that occurred a couple of weeks ago causing considerable consternation in the Ray family. As you know, we both acquired new Taku jackets over the holidays. And the sealskin-soled *mukluks* we have been wearing were Christmas gifts from the mother of one of my little first-graders, "because" as she said, "Gregory like you!"

At any rate, you may recall one of Tod's more onerous tasks is carrying out

---

14. Anthropologists and sociologists have reported instances among the Eskimo clans from Alaska to Greenland in which men are believed to have shared their wives with other men. However, reports of the practice as "hospitality" appear to have been widely exaggerated. Whatever wife-sharing might have taken place is believed to have largely disappeared with the arrival of western missionaries.

the bucket from the chemical toilet and emptying it in the disposal area on the sea ice, where it is carried away in the spring.

As he was about to do this, he came into the house wearing my new jacket. When I asked why he had put on my jacket instead of his own (they both were hanging in the hall outside the door) he replied, "Well, you see, I'm wearing these new *mukluks*. The soles are slippery, and if I fall while carrying the toilet bucket, I certainly don't want to mess up MY new jacket." We both chuckled, but Tod didn't bother to remove my jacket, which he had mistaken for his own. Off he went on his repugnant task.

You can guess what happened. A short time later, Tod came in, having slipped on the ice, with my new jacket fouled by the contents of the toilet. I was livid. "You did this on purpose!" And no amount of reasonable explanation as to why he would have done this to himself could convince me it had been an accident.

Fortunately, the removable outer covering of the jacket was washable, and the jacket has been restored almost to its original condition. In retrospect, we laugh about this episode, considering it to be par for the course of life in an Alaska village.

▲ *Tod and I in our matching Taku jackets and new* mukluks.

I am still busy with my correspondence course. I have only about seven more lessons and I want to finish by the end of January. Then I will sign up for another course. If we don't leave until July, I'll have plenty of time to finish it. Though eager to go, we are looking forward to the spring in Savoonga. Spring and summer are lovely here with the long days and lots of sun. We have only 13 more weeks of school and should be finished by the end of April.

In these "Cold War" days, I feel safer here than I would be sitting in Detroit. I didn't mean to upset you about evacuation plans. Every large city in the States is making the same preparations, and I thought you would be assured to know that we will be ready in case of trouble.

However, I don't believe we have much to worry about. This is not a strategically important spot. Savoonga is more than 40 miles away from either radar station. In case of war, Fairbanks, Anchorage, New York, Detroit, and West Coast ports would be hit first.

Thank you for the egg whites. I use them often. Lee Hittsen, wife of the ship's dentist on the *Health*, also sent me egg whites from Anchorage. I gave some to Helen Pungowiyi for her daughter's birthday cake. Helen is the sweetest woman in the village. I just love her. No, don't send any more Amazo pudding. Maxine and Burton sent a whole carton at Christmas.

Mick Campbell brought us some ground beef on a recent visit. We are running short of fruit juice. However, Alice has plenty, so we are getting juice from her.

Well, I have no more news. Tod is making some Cokes, so we should be refreshed in a minute.

Love, Doris and Tod

❖ ❖ ❖

Friday, January 23, 1953

Dear Mother,

The mail came last night with four letters—one each from you and my aunts. I also received a nice box of candy from my friend Sue McLay. The fruit and coconut balls were delicious. I say "were" because they are all gone already. Tod got a few letters too, so we had an enjoyable evening catching up on the news from home.

The teachers in Gambell sent us a beef roast in payment for some fruit we gave them last summer. We look forward to feasting on it this weekend. Tod has arranged to get about 20 pounds of beef on the next CAA plane. But we don't want to order too much because every so often our weather turns warm and then we must worry about spoilage. We want just enough to give us a break from our canned stuff.

I think Tod will decide to go into elementary-school administration because there is a great demand in that field. Last night, we got an application for an apartment rental at Columbia University. It seems early to be applying, but we surely would like to get into student housing on the campus. It would be so much more convenient. Tod could come home for lunch, and I could, too—if I get a job at the university.

We have had extremely cold weather the past week—down at one point to -30° and hovering around -20° for quite a spell. Today, however, the temperatures are back up to around zero with a raging south wind blowing snow with the consistency of powdered sugar.

There is a storm window in the pantry covered inside with frost, and the unrelenting wind is finding ways to blow the fine snow through the cracks right into the pantry. I'm spending a lot of time in there with a mop. Snow is also packed between the storm and regular windows in the kitchen next to the table where I work. Staying warm is not easy!

Well, I can't think of another thought to squeeze out of this old Underwood typewriter. So, I better take a bath and get ready for bed. Taking a bath means trying to get clean in a thimbleful of water. I think I'll ask Tod to heat some water on the stove so we can enjoy a real bath with ample hot water in one of the galvanized laundry tubs. I could bring the tub into the kitchen by the stove.

I can hardly wait!

Love, Doris

❖ ❖ ❖

Saturday, January 31, 1953

Dear Mother,

Not much is happening here. Only 12 more weeks of school, but January just crept by. We're sticking to our usual schedule of school classes, radio schedules, and various other duties in the villages. We have a holiday on February 22, giving us a long weekend.

The days are getting longer. At this writing, the sun is a big red ball in the sky above the hills—a scene that resembles a lovely landscape painting. It is so good to feel sunshine in the kitchen again.

Tod is collecting Eskimo legends for a project in his language class. Some of the kids are writing reasonably well. We hope to put their Savoonga family stories into booklet form. Others are drawing illustrations. Because Yupik isn't a written language, these English-language booklets will be the only written record of the old stories. We want to make copies for the village families. I'll send you a copy if the project is completed.

Grace has wired a request for flu vaccines. I hope they come on Tuesday's plane. There is an epidemic on the Alaska mainland, and some of our boys are expected back from Nome on Tuesday. We worry they will bring flu germs with them.

I have been making out welfare-investigation forms all day. There seems to be ill-feeling among many in the village about receiving pensions, and we're caught in the middle.

I can't think of anything more to report, and I have lots of work to do. Write soon.
Love, Doris

❖ ❖ ❖

Saturday, February 7, 1953

Dear Mother,

I received your plaintive note that you had not heard from us since Christmas. This surprised me. I feel sure that by the time you receive this letter you will have received all the earlier letters I have written. Even Tod wrote one.

Our mail delivery hasn't been as reliable as it was last year when the plane came on the first and third Tuesdays every month. This year, sometimes the plane comes when it is supposed to but, just as often, it comes a few days late. This irregular schedule causes mail, both incoming and outgoing, to pile up.

Our mail carrier used to mush over the day before the plane was due. This year, he is in no hurry to go because often he must wait in Gambell two or three days for the plane. So, he doesn't go until he hears there is mail in Gambell. That means the plane has already left by the time he gets there, and our mail doesn't go out for another two weeks.

As I write, I am looking at your Mother's Day gift sitting on the windowsill. We got the same thing for Tod's mother. I won't tell you what they are, but I'm sure you will like them. They were made by Teddy Kasake, the carver who made your swans. He is a first-rate artist.

We have been experiencing below-zero weather again. But it has been crisp and clear, too, and we keep quite cozy. It's a beautiful day. I hope we will be able to get out for a walk. As I write, Tod is busy figuring out income taxes. Our W-2 forms came last night. It appears we will have to pay more taxes than were withheld. And then there is the Alaska income tax. Oh, my!

Since Alice recently ordered two old-style upright wall telephones from a magazine advertisement, Tim has been busy trying to string a phone line between the mission and the school. This should be interesting.

Well, that's all I have for now.

Love, Doris

❖ ❖ ❖

Monday, February 16,1953

Dear Mother,

Happy Valentine's Day! A little late. We had a valentine party at school last Friday. What an ordeal! Organizing and putting on classroom parties is a LOT of work for teachers. Thank goodness, we won't have another party until Halloween. The children were busy for weeks making valentine cards. I had some old cards, from which I erased the names, that I gave to the first-graders. They were appreciative!

A little eight-year-old fellow made me a bracelet with a carved ivory heart, held together with elastic. He made it himself, and it was rather crude. He has a lot to learn. But it was the thought behind the gift that moved me. Tim's little girl, Linda, gave me a heart-shaped pin made of white sealskin covered with pins. I'll bet her mother made it.

Tod and I both came down with colds last week and were miserable over the weekend. In fact, Tod didn't teach today. But we feel a lot better now. It's a wonder we didn't catch something sooner with so many kids coughing in our faces.

Only 10 more weeks of school. Yippee! I can't wait for the end of classes and suspect our students feel the same. I am finishing the last lesson in my correspondence course and expecting a new course in the next mail.

Well, better get busy.

Love, Doris

❖ ❖ ❖

Tuesday, February 24, 1953

Dear Mother,

We were so pleased to get three letters and two cards from you today. The mail was late coming. The plane didn't come until Friday. Joseph didn't go over to Gambell until Saturday, and then bad weather held him up. He didn't get back until today. So, we should get more mail in about a week.

We have a new electric popcorn-popper, a Christmas gift from Alice. I am making popcorn now, as Alice and Grace are coming over to see the new color slides that came in today's mail.

The teachers in Gambell sent us 20 pounds of meat—a pot roast, a beef roast, three pork chops, packages of hamburger and stew meat, and some sirloin steak. The cost of all this comes to over $1 a pound plus 10 cents a pound freight between the villages. So, as far as meat deliveries are concerned, I guess this will be it until we go Outside. Speaking of which, we can hardly wait to gorge ourselves when we visit this summer. We're going to be real gluttons, I'm afraid.

Only eight more weeks and two days of school!

We got a chuckle out of your notion that we might visit King and Little Diomede islands on our way back to Savoonga after our summer vacation. You don't realize how difficult it is to travel in this part of the world. Planes get to Diomede between January and April only when the Bering Sea ice is solid enough to support them. And seldom do planes fly to King Island, as they must land on the ice floe. Usually, the King and Diomede islanders gather in Nome or Kotzebue during the summers to carve and sell ivory. They are famous carvers.

Well, it is almost time for school to begin. The days are much longer now. The sun comes up about 7:30 and sets around 5.

Love, Doris

❖   ❖   ❖

Thursday, February 26, 1953

Dear Eunice, H.F., and Boys,

The photos of the boys were grand. My, how they are growing up! We'll hardly recognize them when we come next summer.

We received some color slides back from the film-processor in the last mail. One slide showed two little girls holding a dead white fox on their laps. The fox looks almost alive. The girls were just here to see the slide. They laughed and laughed at themselves. They are such precious children.

We're having a gala celebration of breaded pork chops tonight. We received some fresh meat from the Gambell teachers who were able to get it through CAA. Tod is playing butcher in the kitchen. We decided the pork chops were too thick. Not that we dislike thick chops, but we had to hide them on top of the cupboard so nobody would see them thawing and know we have fresh meat that we have no intention of sharing. So, we will have enough for tomorrow night, too.

After supper: we just finished taking a sunbath. We brought a special bulb with us last year but thought it was broken. The other day we tried it again, and it worked beautifully. So, we hope to have golden tans before too long.

We're counting the days until the school year ends. I'll be so glad when the little monsters go off for the summer. I love them, but the endless winter is making me cranky.

Well, this letter is boring me, too! Write soon.

Love, Doris

❖ ❖ ❖

Thursday, February 26, 1953

Dear Ashfords,

Received your letter and the nice photos of the boys. What a couple of sharpies they are in those bow ties!

This job has its ups and downs, as all jobs do, and recently it has been on the downswing. I worry about the ruination of the villagers by a government pension system designed for people accustomed to a money economy. The Islanders live off the land and sea. Like farmers who derive their livelihood from the land, a big family is an asset in Savoonga.

The old people have a few chores and are not considered a burden. Indeed, the elders are highly respected and well taken care of by their families.

At any rate, the word has gotten out that an old-age pension is available from the territorial government as are grants for aid to dependent children that many of these people qualify for. It makes me sad to see them going hog-wild on the system and substituting their utopian socialism for the greedy, grasping, screw-your-buddy techniques of the capitalist system in which most Americans live.

Being among the few people able to read and write well, we've become unwilling welfare agents. This thankless job is a pain in the neck.

Not only are we increasingly being asked to prepare welfare applications and other forms, but we also must listen to many petty complaints about the system.

The people are split into two groups—those who receive pensions and welfare checks and those who don't. In the first group, there are constant complaints about not getting enough money. In the second are people who do not receive government checks but spend their time snooping into other peoples' business and then bitching about those who do.

I don't mean to imply that Savoonga is unique, though I believe it is more isolated and therefore more independent in the main than most other villages. Still, the trend is changing the culture of villagers whose ancestors for thousands of years have selflessly shared and helped each other.

Believe me, I don't begrudge these hard-working people the niceties of life, nor do I want them to do without things they need. I merely feel that they were happier when they worked for the common good of the village before the emergence of this split-factions situation whereby it is every man for himself.

Enough bitter bantering for now. I am good and ready for a vacation.

Love, Tod

❖　❖　❖

Sunday, March 8, 1953

Dear Mother,

Only seven more weeks of school!

Our mail arrived Friday night and, as usual, we were happy to hear from you. The candy arrived, too, and in good shape. Yum! Much better than the last box. Only a couple of candies, the cherries, were crushed. We are enjoying the candy so much, though at the moment it is in the refrigerator because the living room got over-heated last night.

By the way, before I forget, would you pick up a few things for me at the drugstore? I'd like a can of Dr. Scholl's foot powder, a bottle of cuticle remover, and a tube of Cashmere Bouquet lipstick—medium shade. I just finished one tube and found I have only a little left in the other. I'm also enclosing a copy of current parcel post rates. We are in Zone 8, so anything you send that weighs less than a pound will cost 27 cents. So, if you have a supply of stamps at home, you can wrap packages and put them into a mailbox without having to go into a post office.

Alice is going to Anchorage in about a month. She is going to do two big errands for me—find a crystal for my watch and have a shoe repaired.

Speaking of Alice, she is on a diet. She has been feeding Grace all winter, and, as you know, Grace eats like a horse. She especially likes whipped cream! So, during the winter, Alice gained about 10 pounds. Now they're both on a diet, theoretically. No more desserts and no more eating between meals. I doubt Grace is sticking to her diet, having found candy wrappers in the clinic trash can.

Alice came down the other night, acting as if she was making out her last will and testament. She told us we could have her boxes of Almond Joys and U-No bars (our favorite candy) as she wouldn't be eating them anymore. We had to chuckle, but happily so, as she had three boxes of them.

I have been exercising every night and seem to have tightened my stomach muscles somewhat. I could carry more weight if I could proportion it evenly, but it all seems to settle around my stomach and hips, making me look pregnant.

I'll try to write again before the mail goes out.

Love, Doris

❖ ❖ ❖

Dear Eunice, H.F., and Boys,

Received your latest letter and the photo of my latest nephew. He certainly is a champ, all right—heavyweight division. Of course, we noticed that he was well shod in the little Eskimo skin socks.

We probably mentioned that after one more year here, I plan to go back to school for an advanced degree. Our third year of teaching will allow us to create a "Columbia fund." We figured that with what we can save in a third year, I can attend Columbia University in New York City. Without a doubt, Columbia is the best school in education in the country.

We are so eager that we applied for an apartment on the campus for 1954 and just received a notice that we can have one if I am admitted. What wonderful news this is! Housing has been our biggest worry because apartments are scarce near the university. This means I won't have to commute to school or deal with various other disadvantages of living in a big city. The student apartments are convenient, comfortable, and not too expensive.

The next step is to be admitted, but I can't apply earlier than a year in advance of the date I wish to enroll. So, I'll have to hold up until fall before applying. With Doris working, we should be able to live on her salary and pay for my tuition out of savings. I'm sure we will bend your ears on this subject next summer.

Well, I have numerous letters that should get out, so I'll make this brief. Write when you can.

Love as always, Tod

❖ ❖ ❖

Dearest Mother,

Happy St. Patrick's Day!

Sunday was Tod's birthday, but we celebrated it Saturday night as Alice is busy at the church on Sunday. I bought him some fishing equipment—a fiberglass fly rod and an automatic reel. I sent the money to his brother Burton, who ordered it for me. Grace gave him a fish-cleaning knife, and Alice presented him with a Burl Ives album.

We had fresh meatloaf for dinner. There must have been something wrong with it, however, as all four of us had a touch of indigestion.

I made Tod some raised doughnuts as an extra birthday gift, following Eunice's recipe. I must say in all modesty that they were superb. In fact, I can't remember ever having eaten better doughnuts. I followed the whole recipe but saved half the dough in the refrigerator. Some day this week, I'll take it out, let it rise again, and make some more.

I must inform you, Tod tried in vain to stretch his birthday celebration. He argued that because his birthday came on a Sunday, it should be celebrated on Monday, like government holidays that fall on a weekend. At that, I put my foot down!

We are going to have company in a couple of days. This is top secret! The Air Force is stationing two airmen in Savoonga for a few months. Evidently military men are being stationed in native villages on the Bering Sea to collect intelligence about possible Soviet activities.

With no other place to stay, the airmen will live in Grace's quarters after she moves to Gambell the first of April. Until then, they will be with us. But our pantry is getting low, so I hope the men will bring food with them.

This arrangement is for a couple of weeks only, but it means extra work and inconvenience for us. I guess we'll give them the bedrooms and sleep on the pull-out couch in the living room. This way, we can get up in the morning without disturbing them.

I have no more news, so I'll close for now.

Love, Doris

❖ ❖ ❖

Saturday, March 14, 1953

Dear "Old Lady Derby,"

Thanks for your valentine card with the hint. Yes, I'll try to write occasionally.

Your daughter and I are worn out from a hectic week. Monday started off with a bang—the kids were terrors. We felt dragged out by evening.

Tuesday started out quietly until the afternoon. That was when a little boy was caught fighting in the hall, so Doris made him stay in during recess. More trouble came a little later, just as Doris was returning to the classroom to tell the boy he could go outside for the remainder of the recess. But about that time, the boy's older sister (15, pregnant, not in school) arrived and proceeded to drag her brother from the room.

Doris told the girl she couldn't take him because he was being punished. Hearing this, the sister roundly cursed Doris in Yupik.

I arrived on the scene and tried to talk to the girl. She was in no mood to be reasoned with, so I took the little fellow back into the classroom to a solo accompaniment of more cursing directed at me, this time in English. It was encouraging to hear her speak up so audibly in passable English—something she never had done before as a student.

Anyway, things quieted down the next few days, and we survived another week.

As I am sure you know, we are thoroughly weary of school. I know you must be feeling the same way at your school. We'll all feel better when summer vacation begins. This is a bad time of year, or so it seems. The kids are restless, and we have little energy left. But the end is near!

My correspondence course is bogging down. I hope to get my assignments finished before we leave and then take the final exam when we return. This isn't for credit at Columbia, but is merely education on the elementary level, which I need on this job.

Guess that takes care of my message for this year. Doris will fill in the gaps. Honestly, though, I'll try to be a better correspondent in the future.

Love, Tod

❖ ❖ ❖

Saturday, March 28, 1953

Dear Mother,

I don't have much to report except that the two Air Force men arrived. They have been here about 10 days. Thankfully, they will move into Grace's quarters when she leaves tomorrow. I have been busy feeding them. They are nice fellows and will give us a few more social contacts. Roy Fowler is from Georgia. Jerry Burnsed is from Texas.

I haven't received much mail for over a month, and Tod hasn't fared any better. But I suppose some letters must be on their way to us—slowly.

Well, I'd better get busy. I'll write more later.

Love, Doris

▲ *Nellie Seppilu with her little brother.*

17

Going 'Outside'

■

Terrible news.
When we got into Dutch Harbor
Tuesday night, on our way to Seattle,
a tragic accident delayed the unloading
and set back our departure.

❖ ❖ ❖

Friday, April 3, 1953

Dearest Mother,

The mail came in a little while ago. Everyone, including you, seems to be excited about our forthcoming visit. Eunice said she was trying to arrange a television news interview in Oklahoma City, and Burton is looking forward to a fishing trip.

We received a letter from the ANS area educationalist in Juneau, Max Penrod, informing us that we could count on keeping our jobs next year. I might not have mentioned earlier that we received a formal letter from the ANS personnel department telling us that because we were not certified as elementary school teachers, we could be replaced if the supply of teachers exceeded the demand. Due to this uncertainty, we were anxious about whether to place our annual food order. Then we got the letter from Mr. Penrod saying that our jobs were secure for a third year, which is as long as we intend to stay. So, we are happy!

Major Brown, commanding officer of the Air Force men stationed here, came over from Gambell today on an inspection trip. He brought lots of candy Easter eggs for the children as well as a big box of bubble gum. He gave this to us to distribute. Tod and I immediately divided a share of the bubble gum and now are popping bubbles at each other.

I am going to prepare our grocery order soon. It will come on the fall sailing of the *North Star* for delivery in October. We did not want the order delivered in July, which is considered "spring" here, and then discover we have a year's worth of food but no jobs. With this problem resolved, we can proceed. Because Alice's food order is coming in July, as is Grace's, we can piggy-back a small order onto Alice's order, reimbursing her for the extra cost, and borrow food from her and Grace for repayment in kind next fall.

We are ordering a new kind of canned whole milk for drinking—Meddo Milk. Mick and Betty Campbell sent samples over from Gambell last winter. We were pleasantly surprised to find that it almost tastes like fresh milk. So, we will add two cases to Alice's order and then add 10 or 12 more cases on our fall order.

I forgot to mention that Major Brown also came with about 40 pounds of fresh meat. His boys will take most of it, but he brought some for us, too. We do not want much, as Nome prices are high. When she returns from Anchorage, Alice will bring a box of fresh lettuce, tomatoes, and other vegetables. All this news about fresh meat and vegetables, which we see relatively little of, makes me think I intend to live on a steady diet of steaks, salads, fresh fruit, and milk next summer. Oh, boy!

I'm also looking forward to hearty meals on the *North Star,* made even more delicious by the fact that for two entire weeks I will not have to prepare a single meal or wash a single dish.

When Alice and Grace left on Monday, the Air Force men moved into Grace's quarters, as planned. They are nice fellows, so lonesome for home, but truthfully having them underfoot was bothersome. They are going to pay us $3 a day each for the time they spent with us—about $70 total.

Well, enough for now. I want to read one of the new issues of *Time* magazine.

Love, Doris

❖ ❖ ❖

Saturday, April 11, 1953

Dear Ashfords,

Your well-intentioned offer to arrange a TV interview for us in Oklahoma City doesn't hold the thrill for me that it might. I would be self-conscious and likely would stammer no end. Doris thinks it would be fun, but I'm a born introvert, I guess.

This letter was just interrupted by a village elder who visits frequently. He tells the same stories over and over, but I ooh and aah in the right places every time and never let on I've heard them all before.

His favorite stories are about the time he was attacked by a female walrus that tore the bottom out of his skinboat, the time his wife almost died in childbirth, and the good times he had with friends he met on a construction project on the island.

I can recite the old man's stories from memory, but he enjoys telling them so much that I can't bring myself to cut him short, saying, "Yes, I've heard that story before."

Before I forget, I'll include with this letter a magazine photo of a huge trout that will taunt old Pappy and make his beady little eyes pop.

Nothing more from here. I'll try again soon.

Love, Tod

❖ ❖ ❖

Sunday, April 12, 1953

Dear Mother,

Just TWO MORE WEEKS! By the time you receive this letter, we'll almost be finished. We plan to close school on April 24.

The weather has been balmy. Temperatures are up to about 35-40° during the day, and the ice floe has moved out a little, leaving open water. The skinboat crews have been hunting every day and bringing in a few seals and a couple of walruses.

Clarence Pungowiyi promised Alice that he would take her and me walrus hunting. If I know Alice, she won't let him forget it.

We have been feasting on fresh meat every day for the past week. Major Brown brought us a large supply from Nome. To top it off, Jerry Burnsed, one of the airmen, made a dogsled trip to the Air Force station on Northeast Cape and brought back a sled load of food. The haul included two dozen Birdseye friers and several boxes of frozen steaks and roasts. So, we've been eating steaks, meatloaf, steaks, pork chops, steaks, roast beef, and MORE steaks! Tod is going to fry a chicken this afternoon. He is quite the little chicken-frier.

I am reading *Heaven Is Too High* by Mildred McNeilly and enjoying it greatly. It is a historical novel about the Russian settlement of Kodiak, Alaska, around 1790 under the command of Alexander Andre Andreyevich Baranov.

I just finished the third lesson in my new correspondence course from the University of Washington. The work is going slowly.

Alice has been away almost three weeks but will return to the island on Thursday. Tod says the main reason he'll be glad to see her is that when she arrives, we will have only one more week of school. Isn't that awful?

Guess I'd better close, as I have more letters to write. I always leave them to the last minute before the mail goes out.

Love, Doris

❖ ❖ ❖

Monday, April 20, 1953

Dear Mother,

Our mail came in last night about 9:30, and we were up until midnight reading it. Alice got in about noon today. She and Mick and Betty Campbell, who came from Gambell with her, joined us for dinner tonight. Alice brought me a pastry brush, knowing I wanted one.

The Gambell villagers killed a whale last week, and several dog teams went over to retrieve some of the meat. All the natives will be feasting!

An Alaska National Guard sergeant is visiting Savoonga. He will leave soon, and I have asked him to take this letter to Nome. So, it will get to you sooner rather than later.

Only four more days of school!

Love, Doris

❖ ❖ ❖

Monday, May 4, 1953

Dear Mother,

I should be working on my education course, but on a beautiful spring morning, I just ain't in the mood!

Today begins our second week of vacation—pardon me, I mean second week of doing useful work around the school. Some of the men are painting the building. Last week, I worked on school reports, the inventory, and other bureaucratic tasks, but this week I will get busy on this course.

The days are growing long again. The sun comes up around 3:15 a.m. but the dawn light colors the sky long before then. Sunset is around 8:45, but when we went to bed at 11 last night there was still a rosy glow in the northwest.

I am SO glad that the school year has ended. Of course, we'll have to teach later next spring to make up for a late start this fall. These schedule adjustments are intended to stretch our time Outside this summer. This all came about, as you may recall, because the high cost of flying to Seattle forced us to delay our departure to await passage on the *North Star*, which will stop here in July and then head for Seattle.

I told you about the folks at Gambell getting a whale. They couldn't save all the meat, some of which spoiled on the beach. But the villagers did butcher a couple of tons of blubber and *muktuk*—skin plus attached blubber.

Albert Kulowiyi brought us a little taste, and then Mick and Betty Campbell brought us quite a chunk. *Muktuk* isn't bad, it's just kind of rubbery. To preserve the meat, we emptied all the jars of boric acid from the clinic into one large bag. Then, we filled the little jars with muktuk and pickled it in vinegar, which the Eskimos say is the best way to eat whale.

We filled seven little jars and are sending them to you, Tod's mother, and others in the family. Imagine, you'll get a taste of whale! I hope it goes through the mail without mishap. I'll pack it carefully.

Tod wrote his mother about sending our clothes to you in Detroit. I don't see how we'll be able to tolerate the heat in the States this summer. When it gets up to 70° here, a weather rarity, it is considered a real scorcher. Nothing like Detroit in July. You'll probably have to ladle us into our car and send us off!

Ruth Miklahook had her baby last night. That is the third birth in the village in four days. Tim's wife and another woman both had babies on the same night. Everyone was okay, except Anna bled quite a bit right after her delivery. The midwives sent word to Tod that he should give her a shot of ergotrate. They usually give ergot tablets orally, but Anna's uterus wasn't contracting fast enough, and the ergotrate intravenously works faster. She's all right now.

I must get busy knitting. I have been trying to knit a little something for each new baby, but sometimes I give them a toy instead. The babies are coming fast. Two more are due this month. Those will be the last for a while.

I just finished reading the April *Ladies Home Journal* last night and passed it on to Alice. Still have the *Atlantic, Readers' Digest, and True* magazines to get through. And then I want to get back to some books. Jerry Burnsed lent us a new biography of Edwin Booth, the Shakespearean actor, and *Buddenbrooks*, the novel by Thomas Mann. I want to read both before we leave and would like to finish the Winston Churchill memoir, too. I still have one more volume to read.

Well, I'd better get busy. It is after 10 p.m. I'll write more later, but don't depend on regular mail service from now on. The Air Force is expecting to drop supplies during the breakup season to the fellows here.

Love, Doris

P.S. I saw the first snow bunting bird of the season, and Saturday night we saw the first v-formation of geese flying north. Can spring be far behind?

❖ ❖ ❖

Monday, May 18, 1953

Dearest Mother,

I'm STILL procrastinating work on my education course, so have decided to answer your letters. Eight lessons remain. I want to finish them by the middle of June so I can pack and clean the house before we leave.

Goodness knows when this letter will get out, as no more planes are scheduled to come over for a while. We are hoping that our mail sitting in Nome can be paradropped when the Air Force brings supplies for the fellows here.

Life has been boring the past few weeks. We are so eager to get home. We spoke too soon about the imminent arrival of spring. We have hardly seen the sun, and a constant north wind has kept the ice floe in tight to shore so the men have been unable to hunt. Because meat is becoming scarce, everyone will be glad to see the weather break so hunting can resume.

I received the prettiest Eskimo yo-yo the other night from Helen Pungowiyi. Her husband Clarence said that if anyone in the States wants yo-yos, he and Helen will be glad to make them. Clarence is quite a character. He is aware that the native culture is changing. When he visits, he tells us stories of past life in the village and what the people believed in the old days. And he often suggests subjects for photos that will show Savoonga to people in the States.

Speaking of Clarence, I didn't tell you what happened to the whale *muktuk* we were going to send you. I had packed up the bottles of *muktuk* pickled in vinegar and taken them to the post office. However, the night before the mail was to go over to Gambell, we were called over to Clarence's house. His stomach was terribly upset, and he was vomiting everywhere. The only unusual thing he had eaten had been some *muktuk*.

When it became apparent that he had a touch of ptomaine poisoning, we rushed over to the post office where the postmaster, John Waghiyi, searched through the mail that was bagged up and ready to go. We were able to retrieve the packages of the bottled *muktuk* that we were sending you and others. And that is why you didn't have an opportunity to try whale *muktuk*!

I finally finished *Buddenbrooks* last week and began reading a biography of Nell Gwyn, the English actress who became a mistress of King Charles II. But I put the book aside for a while when the mail brought a fresh stack of *Time* and other magazines.

Well, it's 9:15 a.m. and everyone is busy but me. I have no more news and absolutely MUST work on my correspondence course. More later.

Love, Doris

❖ ❖ ❖

Tuesday, June 9, 1953

Dearest Eunice, H.F., and Boys,

The mail came in Sunday after sitting in Gambell for more than two weeks. The snow on the trail was too soft for dogsleds, and the sea ice hasn't opened all the way down the coast to allow travel by skinboat. The Air Force fellows expect a mail drop this week

Clarence Pungowiyi is going to Northeast Cape tomorrow and is taking our mail with him, so I want to get a note off to you. We won't see any more mail out until the *North Star* comes, and then we won't worry because we'll be on it.

The walrus season has come and gone. It was unusually short this year and late getting started. The first good day for hunting was a week ago Saturday. The villagers made a huge haul. About 15 skinboats set out, and nearly every crew came back with two or more walruses. Tod went with Tim, whose crew brought home three walruses. Tod was thrilled. Then, he went out again one afternoon and believes he got some excellent photos. We'll see. We are impatient to send the film out for processing.

We intend to get a projector in Detroit so we can bore you with our slides. At any rate, hunting was terrific for more than a week. Everyone got all they needed. No more food shortage.

I'm baking a nine-pound ham—a real one! Jerry is going with Clarence to Northeast Cape for about four days. Jerry made a bargain that if I would bake the ham for him, he would give us half of it. And who am I to refuse such an offer? Truthfully, we're so low on food that I have come to dread every meal. Our pantry looks like a store on wartime rations. We drank our last can of fruit juice last week. Our supply of meat is dwindling.

The last we heard, the *North Star* was six days ahead of schedule. However, it might lose time at Hooper Bay because of the difficulty unloading there at low tide. The ship is due here July 1. We're hoping it will be early. The more time it picks up, the longer we'll have in the States. From Seattle, we are going to fly straight to Detroit. After our visit there we will come directly to Oklahoma City to see you.

Love, Doris

❖ ❖ ❖

Sunday, June 21, 1953

Dear Eunice, H. F., and Boys,

I don't think I've told you about the fire.

It happened the same day I last wrote you, and I didn't want to rip the letter open and start over. At about 8:15 p.m., the nurse's quarters in the original school building broke out in flames. Within an hour, the building had burned to the ground. You may recall that two Air Force men were staying in the nurse's quarters there while Grace Crosson was working a rotation in Gambell. Jerry Burnsed was visiting with us at the time. The other fellow was in bed when the fire broke out, but he escaped.

Fortunately, the villagers were able to save a shed containing desks and other school equipment just 30 feet from the fire. Nearly all the men worked together to douse sparks and kept the flames from spreading. We were immensely impressed and grateful for their effort.

Almost nothing was saved from the nurse's quarters. Grace's clothes, ivory, and medical records were destroyed. We haven't heard from her yet, as she is in the States on vacation, but I know she will be sick about this. After the fire, Jerry stayed with us for almost a week. The other airman moved in with a family in the village.

The Air Force tried for several days to get a seaplane into Savoonga. It finally arrived last Sunday with an Office of Special Investigations agent on board, as well as an Air Force captain and Lawrence Williams, the ANS representative in Nome who once taught here. Mr. Williams enjoyed seeing all his Savoonga friends again. They brought first-class mail with them.

We haven't heard anything official but are inclined to believe carelessness caused the fire. The Air Force fellows had a habit of leaving their oil stoves on high, even when they were away. Alice saw black smoke pouring out of the building at 6 that night. Several times before, Tod had gone in and either spoken to the men about the danger of overheating the stoves or had turned them down himself. The ANS has requested us to return home by way of Juneau after our vacation to submit personal reports as to what we saw, and what we know, about the fire.

Meanwhile, the spring voyage of the old *North Star* has been erratic, as usual. It had been six days ahead of schedule, and we were happily anticipating an extra week of vacation. Then, all sorts of things delayed the ship, including a four-day southwest wind that hasn't let up. Because of the weather, the *North Star* couldn't unload at Shaktoolik, so it is back on schedule—for now. If we are lucky, we will dock in Seattle around July 17, fly straight to Detroit, stay there a week or so, and then drive to O.C. But we worry that we might not be able to see everyone this year.

Oh, this dreadful wind is getting me down! At the rate we're going, we'll probably get to Seattle just in time to turn around and come back. Why does this miserable wind have to wreck our lives! (Editorial note from Tod: "Isn't this dramatic?")

Love to you all, and I'll keep you posted.

Love, Doris

❖ ❖ ❖

▲ *Villagers looked on as volunteers fought to save a storage shed from a fire that destroyed the old school. An overheated stove may have been the cause.*

Monday, June 22, 1953

Dear Mother,

We received first-class mail when a seaplane came over to pick up the Air Force fellows after the fire in the old schoolhouse. We should get our second-class mail on the *North Star* and, if so, will have magazines to read on the ship.

Did I tell you that Alice found me two cotton dresses for the trip in one of the mission boxes? They are nice little dresses that I will return to her in the fall. I may be able to pick up another dress on sale Outside, but I don't want to get carried away. I'll be traveling in slacks most of the time.

I think you have my black velvet wedding hat in Detroit. I'm wearing the green hat with the pheasant feather, and I will let you have it, if you can wear it. That darned feather is more trouble than it is worth in Alaska.

I have been awfully busy cleaning the house. I'll write from the ship.
Love, Doris

❖ ❖ ❖

ABOARD THE *NORTH STAR*
Monday, July 6, 1953

Dear Mother,

We are somewhere out on the Bering Sea south of Nunivak Island, which we passed this afternoon. The weather has been surprisingly good so far. The second mate says we may reach Dutch Harbor tomorrow night if the weather remains favorable. We should be in Sitka by Friday or Saturday.

We had quite a time getting away from Savoonga. Bad weather moved in, delaying unloading for 24 hours. Finally, we sailed about 11 a.m. Saturday and anchored off Gambell about 3 p.m. that afternoon. The crew unloaded all that night, and we left Gambell about 24 hours later.

Mick and Betty Campbell came aboard to have lunch with us. We plan to stay with them on our way back.

I fervently hope the sea remains calm, but we hear it may become rough when we pass through the Aleutian Islands and venture out into the North Pacific. We look forward to going ashore in Sitka to visit a few Savoonga patients at Mt. Edgecumbe Hospital. We want to do a bit of sight-seeing in town as well.

The delicious meals on board are everything I hoped for—sirloin steak, roast turkey, hamburger steak, and spareribs, with all the trimmings. But I'm eating too much!

Our stateroom is clean and comfortable—bunks on one side (Guess who has

▲ *Tod fed Rupert, a Siberian husky outcast from the Air Force station.*

the top bunk?), a settee on the other side, a dresser in between, and a bathroom with a SHOWER!

This afternoon we watched a movie, *Callaway Went Thataway*, a comedy western starring Fred McMurray and Dorothy McGuire. Not bad.

While we are away, Alice will take care of Rupert, the husky orphan we recently adopted. Yes, I know what you are thinking—what about our decision not to have a dog? Well, our resolve weakened when we found Rupert—or, rather, he found us.

The commander at the Air Force station had evicted Rupert, an Air Force mascot, due to concern about the hydatid disease. Rupert was spoiled, having been fed steaks and receiving much attention. He was given to a musher who tied Rupert to his dogsled for the return to Savoonga.

Evidently, Rupert was not used to a leash and running alongside a dogsled, so whenever the musher stopped to rest Rupert jumped up onto the sled. Later, Rupert got loose and ended up on our doorstep. We took him in, and he soon ruled the roost.

Alice is not fond of dogs, but Rupert seems to have taken a liking to her. Whenever she comes down to visit, Rupert insists on walking her home and then returning to the school.

▲ *Tod fed the offspring of Rupert, the charming dog*
we had told ourselves we would never have.

The plan was for him to stay at the school, where Alice would feed him once a day.

However, soon after we boarded the ship, Alice sent us a note reporting that when she returned home after seeing us off, she found Rupert on her doorstep. So, she guessed she'd have to bring his food to her quarters. We chuckled, knowing how she feels about dogs. But I am confident Rupert will be in good enough hands until we return.

Enough for now. Detroit, here we come!

Love, Doris

❖ ❖ ❖

ABOARD THE *NORTH STAR*
Sunday, July 12, 1953

Dear Mother,

Terrible news. When we got into Dutch Harbor Tuesday night, on our way to Seattle, a tragic accident delayed the unloading and set back our departure.

A family from Gambell had been aboard, traveling to Dutch Harbor. The crew was about to lower a lifeboat to take them ashore. But just as the woman stepped into the boat, the ropes came loose, and the boat dropped into the water. The woman fell with the boat and was killed when it hit the water. What a horrible scene! Since the family is related to several Savoonga villagers, I felt I should write to them describing the accident. Not easy to do!

We have had poor weather the past couple of days, and we have lost more time. Not much activity on board the past couple of days. We've seen three movies since leaving Gambell. I'm surely looking forward to getting ashore in Sitka tomorrow. We should be there in 12 hours or so.

Love, Doris

❖ ❖ ❖

SITKA, ALASKA
Saturday, July 13, 1953

Dear Mother,

Last night, we went to bed around midnight but couldn't sleep. I got up about 3 a.m.

Through a porthole I saw a shadowy mountain landscape and the lights of Sitka in the distance. We dressed and climbed up onto the main deck. Mo, the second mate, was standing watch in the pilot house and yelled for us to join him. From there, we had a spectacular view. We were enchanted by the scenery as the ship entered Sitka Harbor just as the sun was rising behind the nearby mountains.

We tied up about an hour ago, at 4:45 a.m. Shortly after, the superintendent of the Mt. Edgecumbe Hospital came aboard with the ship's mail, which to our great surprise included THREE letters from you.

Sitka is one of the most beautiful places I have ever seen. It is nearly surrounded by jagged, snow-capped peaks that come right down to the water's edge. There is a narrow waterway between Sitka on the mainland and the Mt. Edgecumbe school and hospital on Japonski Island, which was a naval base during the war. A fishing port of about 4,600 people, Sitka was the capital of Alaska before the territory's purchase from Russia in 1867.

We'll be here about 12 hours and will spend much of that time ashore. We'll go into town first to see the Tlingit totem poles and the Russian St. Michael the Archangel Cathedral. This afternoon, we will visit several Savoonga patients at Mt. Edgecumbe Hospital. We'll also look up some friends of Alice at the Sheldon Jackson School.

Rumor has it we may travel south through the Inside Passage rather than back out into the North Pacific. That would be grand—smoother sailing, more scenery.

By the time you get this letter, we'll be close to Seattle. I hope we get in on Friday early enough to catch a plane that night from Seattle-Tacoma Airport. See you soon.

Love, Doris

18

Stateside Summer

*Mother gorged us
with as much fresh food
as we could eat—bacon,
lettuce, and tomato sandwiches,
salads galore, and all kinds
of berries. What a treat!*

❖ ❖ ❖

GRAND JUNCTION, COLORADO
Sunday, August 16, 1953

Dear Alice and Grace,

I hope you can share this letter, as I want to bring you up to date on our travels, visits with relatives, and plans for returning to Savoonga. I hope it will arrive before we do, but one never knows during the summer months.

We arrived in Seattle on July 18 and flew to Detroit the next day. We had a wonderful reunion with my mother.

Icing on the cake: When they heard of our imminent arrival, my Aunt Evelyn Hamill ("Auntie Wun") and cousin Bobbie drove down from their home in Blind River, Ontario, and were staying with my Aunt Gladys Shepley in Winsor, just across the Detroit River from Detroit.

They all descended on us the next day for a grand get-together. We immediately made plans for a picnic and swimming at a park on the shores of Lake Erie—which we carried out a few days later.

Mother gorged us with as much fresh food as we could eat—bacon, lettuce, and tomato sandwiches, salads galore, and all kinds of berries.

What a treat! (I hope I'm not rubbing a sore spot. I promise, we will bring back some fresh food from Nome in late August.)

With a little more than a month to cross the country and visit as many of Tod's relatives as possible, we couldn't remain with my family for too long.

Tod got a good tip from his brother John, a mechanical engineer who had been talking to the Ford Motor Company about a possible job. It seems that Ford has a program of providing drivers with expenses to drive new cars from the factory in Detroit to various parts of the country. When we checked with Ford, we learned the company had a new sedan ordered for delivery to Dallas, Texas, just 200 miles or so from Oklahoma City—our next destination. What luck!

So, after about 10 days in Detroit, catching up with my mother and with my aunts and a cousin who came back and forth from Windsor, off we went in a brand-new Ford sedan for a cross-country trip. We had a week to make it to Dallas.

We arrived in Oklahoma City a couple of days later and were captured in bear-hugs by Eunice, H.F., and the nephews. And, of course, we were thrilled to greet our newest nephew, Alan, a charming and adorable eight-month-old. Also, we saw Tod's sister Hazel and her two children who had driven from Clovis, New Mexico, to see Tod and meet me for the first time.

Tod continued the drive to Dallas and returned by air to O.C., a round-trip completed in a day. Nephew Jimmie volunteered to accompany Tod on the drive and took his first airplane ride. While they were gone, Eunice and Hazel entertained me with a trip to the Oklahoma State Museum, a delicious luncheon of more fresh goodies, and an opportunity to become better acquainted. When we picked up the travelers at the airport, Jimmie was proudly sporting a special pilot's badge that he had received while visiting the cockpit on the flight from Dallas. What a special day!

A few days later, after Hazel returned to New Mexico, Eunice suggested that Tod and I borrow her car for a drive to western Colorado to pick up some belongings that Tod had left in their mother's home as well as several mementoes, including a desk, that Eunice wanted. Tod's brother Burton was getting the house ready for sale. (You will recall Tod's mother died earlier in the year.)

The drive to Colorado took several days. We were able to load Eunice's desk half into the trunk and tie it down. The rest of the car was filled with Tod's "junk" and Eunice's mementoes. When we arrived back in O.C. and pulled up to the Ashford home one evening, we noticed an unfamiliar car in the yard and wondered if they had guests. However, we soon learned that we had acquired a new possession—a pre-war Dodge sedan that H.F. had purchased for us somewhere and somehow!

After a few more days visiting with the Ashford family and being plied with fresh produce and Tod's favorite foods—including okra—we were off in our new second-hand car, this time back to Colorado for a brief visit with Tod's brothers John and Burton and their families in the Denver area. Then, we would head west.

I must tell you the okra story before I get too far away from O.C. Not being familiar with southern cooking, I had never tasted okra. Because it was a favorite vegetable of Tod's, Eunice often added it to the menu—typically boiled and served with butter. I'd take a bite, try to swallow it, would get it down, and back up it would come. I'd try again. Same result. How embarrassing! I didn't like okra much but tried to be polite. Finally, it became evident that I was not capable of swallowing boiled okra, so Eunice then switched to okra dipped in cornmeal and fried. That was better—not particularly good, but better!

I have a special relationship with our nine-year-old nephew Jimmie. He loves to tease me. After my okra "problem," he would delight in cuddling with me, wrap an arm around me, and suggest, "Aunt Doris, how would you like a nice big serving of boiled okra? It would be so-o-o good!" This became Jimmie's favorite way of teasing me. Being a good sport, I would react with horror, much to his delight.

Monday night—in a motel somewhere in Nevada:

Well, I've been working on this letter for long enough. It goes into the mail tomorrow morning. Driving through the Nevada desert in August is miserable— hot, hot, hot, even with every window rolled down. However, we have been noshing on fresh peaches and cherries we picked up in western Colorado. We're on our way to Carmel, California, to visit Tod's brother Ken and sister-in-law "Cille." Then we will head up the coast to Seattle.

We intend to put the car into storage in Seattle during the coming school year and then will drive it back across the country, revisiting family on the way to New York. We expect to fly to Nome via Fairbanks on Pan American and arrive back in Savoonga by the end of August. The next year promises to be a long one away from family members we miss.

I hope Rupert has been behaving himself and not causing too much inconvenience. And I hope you both have enjoyed a pleasant summer. We have had a wonderful time back home but are looking forward to seeing everyone in Savoonga soon.

And now to sleep—and then onward toward California tomorrow!

Love to you both, Doris (and Tod)

19

Back to Savoonga

◼

*Our glimpse of
the outside world left us
rather discontented. Next summer,
we likely will be ready to return
to so-called "civilization,"
high prices and all.*

❖ ❖ ❖

SAVOONGA
Wednesday, September 9, 1953

Dear Mother,

We started school yesterday, but today was our first full day. So far, nothing much has happened.

We flew from Nome to Gambell on Friday, August 28. The next morning, we left for Savoonga in a skinboat, but the weather turned bad after we had been

▲ *Clarence Pungowiyi and his crew pushed off to fish in the Bering Sea.*

underway for about an hour. We had to turn back. We couldn't leave again until Tuesday, September 1. Were we ever glad to get home!

We spent the rest of the week getting things in shape to begin school. Our custodian, Albert Kulowiyi, is on leave this week and will be away for three weeks, so we (that is, Tod) have lots of extra chores around the school such as pumping fuel oil.

Our glimpse of the outside world left us rather discontented. Next summer, we likely will be ready to return to so-called "civilization," high prices and all. Our food tastes terrible after we gorged ourselves all summer. Even Alice seems harder to tolerate. Mick Campbell came over from Gambell to spend a week here, so he will probably take Alice off our hands for a while. I guess we're just grumpy, that's all. We are more than happy that Alice is our neighbor and friend.

Judging from his tail-wagging, Rupert was exceedingly happy to see us. But we were sorry to learn we can't take him with us when we leave. In Juneau, we consulted a veterinarian who told us the Territory's quarantine of dogs on St. Lawrence Island was permanent, and that no exceptions could be made. However, Grace has taken a liking to Rupert, so we guess he will have a home here. This situation saddens us, but we realize that Rupert likely would not have been happy living in a New York City apartment.

Tod was just talking to our friends Bill and Beatyann Rasmussen, who taught on King Island last year. We saw them in Nome. Beatyann just learned she is pregnant. Bill told Tod they are transferring to Rampart, an Indian village on the Yukon River about 80 miles northwest of Fairbanks. I was glad to hear the news, as there is no plane service to King Island. There is no road to Rampart, but our friends will be able to fly easily to and from Fairbanks. We are sorry Bill and Beatyann will be too far away to talk to by short-wave radio, as we have enjoyed our over-the-air visits in the evenings.

Betty Campbell in Gambell is pregnant, too, and on top of that she and Mick have adopted an adorable, half-Yupik baby. Betty certainly will have her hands full this winter. It seems as if everyone we know is pregnant. Hope the condition isn't contagious.

The skinboat that brought Mick may go back tomorrow, so I will have him mail this letter in Gambell.

We look forward to the arrival of the *North Star* in mid-October. I'm also eagerly awaiting our new phonograph records, current magazines, and other mail. Oh, and more food, too!

All for now.

Love, Doris

❖ ❖ ❖

▲ *Tod amid the ice and snow.*

Sunday, October 4, 1953

Dear Mother,

It is a lovely, bright Sunday morning. We just finished listening to Red Barber's colorful play-by-play broadcast of the Brooklyn Dodgers losing a game to the NY Yankees in the World Series. The winds are brisk, and the waves are crashing dramatically on the beach.

I had your skin socks washed and a gusset sewn in so you will be able to pull them on more easily. They look like new. I must have ours washed before we leave next spring.

We have had no mail since we left Nome. The *North Star* is unusually late this fall. It has been anchored off Nome for two weeks awaiting the arrival of an Alaska Steamship vessel that is bringing lumber and other building materials for Grace's new living quarters here and in Gambell. I'll bet the construction crew is upset by the long delay. Our boss, Max Penrod, is in Nome, too, awaiting transportation to the Island for school visits.

Evidently the *North Star* will not leave Nome before the eighth or ninth and, even with good weather, won't be here before the fifteenth. And good weather is unlikely. At this time of year, I suspect the ship will be fighting storms. Meanwhile, we are running short of food.

Do you remember me writing about the boy who was sent to a sanitorium with a severe case of tuberculosis and a withered arm? After seeing him at Mt. Edgecumbe last summer, we came away fearing he wouldn't live long.

A few days ago, we received a telegram reporting that the boy, Morris Toolie, is being discharged and will arrive in Nome in time to return home on the *North Star*. You can imagine what joy this news brought to his parents, Jimmie and Mabel Toolie.

Unfortunately, we have had a north wind for several days. The Bering Sea has been too rough for skinboats, preventing Grace from traveling to Savoonga. Her plan is to come on the first fair-weather day and stay until the *North Star* stops on its way to Gambell. She will stay with us. This worries me. Our food supply is so low that I don't know how I'll be able to cater to her ravenous appetite.

Last night, Clarence Pungowiyi came for a visit and spent most of the evening. Alice was here, too.

I finally finished *Hearth in the Snow* by Laura Jones, the ANS supervisor who visited us last year. We both consider it to be among the best books we've read about Alaska. Now I want to finish *Crusade in Europe* by Dwight Eisenhower.

We are busy trying to keep the school in good shape for Max Penrod's visit. He expects to come over on the *North Star*.

Tod is about to submit his application to Columbia University. If he decides to go there next fall, we will stop in Detroit at the end of the summer on our way to New York.

Write soon and often. I'll be glad when our regular mail service begins in November. (Or December, or January!)

Love, Doris and Tod

P.S. I'm having trouble writing. Rupert wants to play and is chewing a slipper to get my attention. He has been full of life all evening.

❖ ❖ ❖

Sunday, October 18, 1953

Dear Mother,

The *North Star* anchored offshore last night, but the water has been too choppy for unloading to begin. This morning, a single skinboat went out about

7:30 to pick up a few of the passengers and bring in the first-class mail. FINALLY, we received some letters.

It is now 10:30 a.m. The water looks calmer, so we expect unloading to begin shortly. We'll be so grateful to get our resupply of food, especially the reindeer meat and 15 dozen fresh eggs at about $1.25 per dozen.

Mr. Penrod did not come in this morning, but we may see him this afternoon. Truthfully, we hope that if the weather worsens, he will remain on board. Otherwise, he might get stuck ashore and have time to observe us teaching. That is the LAST thing we want!

Well, I'd better cut this short and get the house tidied up.

Love, Doris

❖ ❖ ❖

Wednesday, October 21, 1953

Dear Mother,

More news about the *North Star*. On Sunday afternoon, the men decided to try to unload the ship. Mr. Penrod came ashore and spent the afternoon with us.

Mr. Penrod seemed pleased by everything he saw at the school. He kept saying, "There must be something you are hiding. It just can't be this good." He said that offhand he could name at least 10 places he'd like to send us to run the school as we have here. Later, he asked Tod if he'd be interested in an administrative position. So I guess he was satisfied. He said it was a rare treat to go to a school and just sit, visit, and drink coffee with the teachers instead of having to listen to a litany of complaints.

Unloading was completed in three hours. We went out to the ship with Mr. Penrod but didn't stay long because the last skinboats were beginning to return to shore.

We worked all day Monday unpacking our food and putting it away. Tod butchered our reindeer, and we had reindeer steaks that night. Alice got a new refrigerator with a large freezer compartment. So, she got a quarter of the reindeer. I hope that will keep us in fresh meat for most of the winter.

I've just heard that Nelson Alowa is going to Northeast Cape, so I will send this letter with him. Our other mail went out on the *North Star* and likely will not reach Seattle until sometime in November.

That's all for now. Write soon.

Love, Doris and Tod

20

Measles Epidemic

We were shocked upon
entering one-room homes to find rows
of sick people wrapped in sleeping bags
and other bedding spread out
across the floor.

Monday, November 9, 1953

Dear Mother,

We have been on the run the past week making sicks calls due to a measles epidemic. We have about 50 cases, and more villagers are becoming sick every day. We don't know how much longer we will be able to keep school open.

▲ Tod was in frequent radio contact with an ANS doctor during the epidemic.

Grace is in Gambell, fighting the epidemic there, too. Fortunately, Tod and I are "measled," as Clarence Pungowiyi put it, meaning we don't have to worry because we both had measles when we were children. If it gets much worse, we may reduce school hours to morning only.

My six little first-graders are caught up with their schoolwork, and I don't want to start anything new while some children are absent. So, the six are working on jigsaw puzzles for the last 15 minutes of class as I write this.

We have had good weather for a week except for occasional high winds. I'll be glad when Troutman Lake freezes solidly enough for planes to land at Gambell. The last we heard the lake was about 12 inches thick, half the thickness needed to support airplanes. We hope the winter planes start coming before December.

We finally got through the magazines that came on the *North Star* and have turned to our new books. I am reading a history of England from the time of the Norman Conquest until the signing of the Magna Carta. The details of medieval life are fascinating.

Wednesday is a welcome holiday, though we'll have lots of sick calls to make.
Love, Doris & Tod

P.S. No mail is going out so I can add a note. The mail carriers are ill. The epidemic is spreading fast! At least 190 villagers have been sick. We've had to close school and are busy with medical calls. One little boy died. I will write you about it when I can. Don't worry about us.

❖ ❖ ❖

Monday, November 22, 1953

Dear Mother,

We are so thankful the measle epidemic is behind us. It was a terrible ordeal for everyone. I haven't had time before now to write you about our experience.

The epidemic of rubeola-virus ("red") measles broke out in Savoonga and Gambell after visits by the *North Star*.

With no natural immunity, the only villagers not susceptible to the disease were elders who had survived a measles epidemic brought to Savoonga by whaling ships about 60 years ago.

As the epidemic spread, Tod and I divided the village between us and made twice-daily rounds. We were shocked upon entering one-room homes to find rows of sick people wrapped in sleeping bags and other bedding spread out across the floor. Soon this scene became commonplace as we did our best to care for everyone. In the evening, we would return to check on those most seriously ill.

Tod was the "doctor" and carried the official medical bag. As "doctor-substitute," I filled an over-the-shoulder handbag with medications and supplies including thermometers, alcohol for disinfectant, and individually wrapped penicillin shots.

Tod maintained short-wave radio communications twice a day with the Alaska Native Service representative in Nome. He also spoke often with a doctor at the ANS hospital in Kotzebue who gave us instructions for the care of the measles patients.

We quickly learned there was little to be done for most patients other than provide aspirin, keep their rooms dark, and ensure they remained indoors and got plenty of rest. The ANS doctor in Kotzebue recommended a shot of penicillin and alcohol bath—rubbing the body with an alcohol swab to cool it—for patients whose temperature rose dangerously high.

However, our supply of penicillin ran low. No one in the village was well enough to make a dogsled trip to Gambell for more. Health authorities in Nome attempted an airdrop, but the drop missed its mark, landing far out of reach on the sea ice.

After making house calls all day and into the night, Tod and I literally fell into bed, exhausted. On more than one occasion, we were wakened by a villager who had entered our quarters and was standing over our bed, flashlight in hand, gently shaking Tod awake. The villager urged him, "You come now," explaining that someone was seriously ill. Wearily, Tod would get up, dress, go off to see the patient, and return later to his warm bed for another few hours of sleep.

Mother, we were lucky to have had just one death, but we treated many life-threatening cases. One of the most serious was that of a little girl barely a year old, whose parents, Joseph and Katherine Noongwook, had brought her back to the village from a trapping camp. First, on top of the measles, she developed pneumonia, then her temperature soared. The doctor said she should be given alcohol rubs every four hours.

Tod would visit the child to give alcohol rubs throughout the day and again just before our bedtime around 10 in the evening. Returning home, he would set his alarm for 1:45 a.m. to go back for another alcohol rub. The first time Tod returned at 2 a.m. the parents were surprised and somewhat annoyed at being awakened in the middle of the night. The little girl was so ill she was just lying quietly, not even crying.

Exasperated, Tod explained, "Baby is VERY ILL. Her temperature is 107.8°. When temperature goes to 106°, people usually die. I MUST keep her cool." This got their attention. They were grateful when they understood how serious the situation was.

One uncommon sight during the epidemic gave us a weary chuckle. With so many villagers ill and unable to do their daily chores, it became the task of several elders (who had survived measles many years before and were immune to it) to carry their family "honey-buckets" and empty them onto the shore ice at the mouth of the frozen creek. This onerous task usually was assigned to younger members of the family, typically girls or women. And certainly not to elderly men, the village leaders!

I am so relieved and happy that all this is behind us. More news later.

Love, Doris

❖ ❖ ❖

Friday, December 4, 1953

Dear Mother,

The mail finally arrived!

Our mail got as far as Gambell on November 20, but no one could go after it during the measles epidemic. Dennis Pungowiyi finally was able to go over last Saturday. He started back on Tuesday, December 1, but didn't get far.

For four days, Dennis was stuck at a trapping camp halfway between the two villages waiting out a severe wind and snowstorm. He made it in about 4:30 this afternoon. I just finished reading all our letters and am keyed up, so will try to get a note off to you.

You asked when we will leave next summer. Before we go, we must make up the two weeks we lost during the epidemic. Our teaching contract provides transportation back to the States at ANS expense. We don't know yet whether we will fly out or be taken to Seattle on the *North Star*. My guess is we will leave sometime in July.

Tod and I have resolved not to make premature plans as we did last year, disappointing us when they don't turn out. Much will depend on whether Tod goes to graduate school at Columbia. We should hear in the next mail or two whether he has been accepted.

All that talk in your letters of beautiful fall weather makes me colder than ever. The temperature was down to -2° this morning. Tod got up in the night for the old down comforter, so we were nice and warm—until we got up. The house felt icy cold! I rushed out, put the coffee on, then jumped back into bed for a few extra minutes.

I have sad news. Yesterday, we learned that our dog Rupert had been shot near a fox trap. It is common for the villagers to shoot loose dogs near their traps because the dogs destroy valuable fox pelts. The fellow who shot him didn't know it was Rupert.

We were both sick about it, but we have no one to blame but ourselves. We should have tied him up, but we never dreamed he'd run so far from the village. Rupert was the most intelligent and affectionate pet I've ever known. I want to cry every time I think of him.

Guess I'd better close for now.

Lots of love, Doris

❖ ❖ ❖

December 9, 1953

Dear Mother,

Tod got a postcard from Columbia confirming receipt of his application for grad school and letting him know he will be advised soon whether he will be accepted. It will be a relief to know where we will be in the fall.

I'm sorry to hear that you may be alone for Christmas. Why not come to Savoonga and join us for a canned-chicken feast! I wish you could visit. It would be an exciting, eye-opening experience for you. However, I wouldn't wish on you the ordeal of making an eight-hour dogsled trip over from Gambell. Anyway, we'll be thinking of you at Christmas, as always, and wishing YOU were here instead of the Presbyterian missionary.

I'm enclosing a complimentary letter that our boss, Max Penrod, wrote to us. After you read it, please return it. Tod wants to attach a copy of it with his job applications after grad school.

There is a slight possibility we may transfer to another ANS school, but only if Tod receives a lucrative offer. But we wouldn't want to transfer to another isolated village. We might be tempted if we were offered Unalakleet, Kotzebue, Barrow, Fort Yukon, Hydaburg, or Angoon—with good money.

We might consider teaching in an Indian school in the States. Most BIA schools are in Arizona and New Mexico among the Navajo, Apache, and other tribes, and in North and South Dakota.

The planes are coming to Gambell the first and third Fridays this winter. That is ideal for us as it means mail should get to Savoonga by Saturday or Sunday. We dislike getting letters on weeknights, as we usually get keyed up from reading them and can't get to sleep. Last night's first-class mail was rather disappointing. Not too many letters, and a lot of our magazines are still in Gambell.

Guess it is time for the last bell, and I'd better get my hair combed.

Love, Doris

❖ ❖ ❖

Saturday, December 26, 1953

Dear Mother,

We had a nice enough Christmas, but I'm surely glad it's over. I can hardly wait until we are on our way home. But these next five or six months will certainly drag.

I love the pretty yellow nightie you sent. Thank you so much. Tod seemed enchanted when I wore it Christmas night. He hates those old flannel pajamas I begged from you last summer. I'm sure those PJs must have been too big for you. They look like a clown suit on me. But I am grateful for them and expect to wear them until I leave.

Tod speaks of throwing them away and ordering new ones, but I don't want to buy any more flannels as I won't wear them in the States.

We got our usual box of food from Burton and Maxine. I guess she didn't know that Philadelphia Cream Cheese is perishable. She enclosed three or four packages of it in a bag of candy and dates. Of course, everything was moldy. We threw the whole bag away. Elsewhere in the box were cellophane snack bags of fruit and nuts, which we enjoyed. However, we'll be glad to get back to the States, so we won't receive food gifts at Christmas. Most of the foods we already have, and the postage is expensive.

Alice gave us a record with music from *Swan Lake*, the Russian ballet. Grace gave Tod an autographed copy of a new history of Alaska by a professor at the University of Alaska. She also gave Alice and me wicker baskets with little cloth pockets for hot rolls. I'll have to talk Alice into making some rolls for us.

We received an assortment of gifts from the villagers, including a fox pelt and four or five ivory letter-openers. It seemed as if just about every package we opened had a letter-opener. Tod brought out his gift for me—another letter-opener! We just howled. This happens every year. The first year we got dozens of pickle forks, and Tod had bought me a pickle fork. Last year, I got several pairs of slippers and boots, and he had bought me a new pair of boots.

I received fancy belts from two village women, and we got quite a bit of fine ivory. Teddy Kasake, the man who carved your duck and swans, gave us two little swans. I was so pleased, as we didn't have any of our own. Tod also received an elaborate cribbage board.

I must go into the classrooms and help put away the desks, so will close for now. Love, Doris

❖ ❖ ❖

Monday, December 28, 1953

Dear Granny,

Christmas is over, and we are glad to get the mess of our program and all the accompanying confusion behind us. We have lost much of the Christmas spirit, mainly because of the mountain of work at school that goes with it. It used to be easy to feel the spirit of Christmas when we were kids, and our mothers did all the work to make sure we enjoyed the season. All we had to do was open our gifts and have fun!

Thank you for the records, which are among our favorites. Let's consider one of the records to be for my birthday. You have given us such nice things, but we don't want you to do too much.

We are observing a controversy in the village that is causing much haggling and trouble. A large barge, more than 200 feet long, somehow broke away from a tugboat at sea and drifted onto the beach 10 miles east of here. One of the village men came upon it. No one here is familiar with salvage laws, though a lawyer in Nome is quoted as saying it is a case of "finders-keepers." There are opposing views, of course.

It is a valuable haul. Found aboard the barge were a brand-new GMC pickup truck, 5,000 gallons of stove oil, a quantity of gasoline, and a large supply of building materials, among other things.

The salvage value is estimated at more than $10,000.[15] The man who found the barge intends to claim it and all contents for himself. Other villagers, envious of the finder, want to share the bounty without waiting for legal clarifications. We have no idea how this will end.

We are still awaiting word from Columbia University. Our plans are indefinite because we aren't certain where we will be next year. Doris probably told you that we haven't completely given up the idea of transferring to another school, but a move seems unlikely. Our boss said he would fix us up with something good, but we doubt his definition of "good" would agree with ours.

That's all for now. Write when you have time.

Love, Tod

---

15. Adjusting for inflation, worth about $112,000 in 2023.

▲ *Tod and Jonathan Annogiyuk spent a week searching for reindeer.*

Reindeer
Perspective: Imported reindeer a temporary substitute for walruses

IN THE LATE 1800s, Dr. Sheldon Jackson, a Presbyterian missionary and territorial agent for the U.S. Department of Education, was distressed to learn the extent of food shortages discovered among the native peoples in western Alaska, including St. Lawrence Island.

On St. Lawrence, a famine from 1878 and 1880 killed a large percentage of the island's population, at that time estimated at around 4,000.[16] The Eskimos were unable to feed themselves due to disastrously low populations of walruses—their primary food supply.

Jackson arranged for the import of domestic reindeer from Lapland to coastal areas of the mainland and brought herders to teach the native peoples how to tend to the herds. The reindeer for St. Lawrence Island came from nearby Siberia.

In 1900, the U.S. government imported 1,280 of the animals from across the Bering Sea, and a herders' camp was established. By 1917, the herd is said to have grown to more than 10,000 animals. The village of Savoonga was established near the camp in the 1930s.

Over the years, however, the reindeer population declined for reasons that are not entirely clear. The Eskimos preferred living in the village to tending the herd. Eventually the hunters returned to the Bering Sea in search of their favorite traditional food—walrus.

In the early 1950s, the Alaska Native Service proposed to revive the island's reindeer industry. Tod was directed to count the remaining animals to determine whether there were enough to form a new herd. This was something of a mystery. We recalled reading an encyclopedia article reporting that the island had a large herd, though we had not seen a single reindeer since our arrival.

In the spring of 1954, Tod and Jonathan Annogiyuk spent a week searching the 90-mile island by dogsled. No reindeer were found. ANS gave up on the reindeer project.

---

16. The island's 2020 population was 1,475.

▲ *Tod scanned the landscape for signs of reindeer.*

21

Final Months

*Yesterday I traveled to
Gambell by dogsled with Clarence Pungowiyi.
We had a smooth trip, covering 60 miles in
seven hours—good time.*

❖ ❖ ❖

Sunday, January 3, 1954

Dear Mother.

I have good news. Tod got his acceptance letter from Columbia today. We are thrilled! I'm going to write immediately to confirm that we want to take the campus apartment that we were offered.

Also, the mail brought two fat letters from you. My, but it felt comforting to hear from you again. Happy New Year!

We have two guests staying with us—Mick Campbell and an Alaska National Guard sergeant. So, I seem to be doing nothing but preparing meals and washing dishes.

We expected them yesterday. But they didn't get in until 2:30 this morning. They told us it was a miserable trip. The sergeant's feet were frostbitten. Seems the dog teams wandered off the trail and got lost in the hills. The trip took about 20 hours, twice longer than it should have. We fixed a meal for the weary travelers in the wee hours, then we all slept until about 10 a.m.

Mick brought us a dozen fresh oranges, a treat that we will share with Alice.

I'm glad you had such a fine Christmas. I was worried about you being alone. I suppose you received my letter by now telling you about our Christmas. I'll be glad to spend it elsewhere next year.

Grace Crosson will be coming back to Savoonga in a couple of weeks, just as soon as her new quarters are ready. It will be a welcome change for Tod not to have to make sick calls at all hours, but the nurse with the vociferous appetite presents another problem. She holds a clinic in the school each afternoon and usually migrates to our quarters about mealtime. We feel we must invite her to join us for dinner. But we do understand she is lonesome and don't mind too much.

We may not leave until late June, or even July. To make up for school cancellations caused by the measles epidemic, we will have to teach until the end of May, and possibly longer if the walrus season starts before then. Then, during breakup in June, we won't be able to get to Gambell to catch a flight to Nome. It will be too late to get there by dogsled and too early to make the trip in a skinboat. We may wait for the *North Star*, which is due in July.

Whichever way we go, the ANS will pay our way to Seattle. We want to get there as soon as possible to start our vacation.

I seem to have run down for now but will write more later. I just finished the lunch dishes, and its already time to start dinner.

Love, Doris and Tod

❖ ❖ ❖

Monday, January 18, 1954

Dearest Mother,

The mail came in this morning about 10. The dogsled team left Gambell at midnight and traveled all night under a beautiful full moon. We spent most of the noon hour reading letters—I almost skipped lunch. We weren't much in the mood to go back to school at 1 p.m.

I'm going to send my fox pelt to you. Would you mind having it tanned? You may as well leave it in storage, too, so moths won't get into it. Please let me know how much this costs. I will send you a check.

We both have been well this winter. I did have one minor cold, and Tod wasn't sick at all. The only thing plaguing us is acute boredom. Time is dragging by. Each week seems to go by more slowly than the one before. Have I mentioned that I can hardly wait until the end of June?

In the last mail, I sent out a few job applications to New York City—to Columbia University, *Time* magazine, and the United Nations. I hope I get something stimulating.

We haven't taken many photos this year, mostly of the puppies that Rupert sired. We also took flash photos of an Eskimo dancing performance by a few of the older men at school.

Yesterday I did a washing, as all our sheets were dirty. The utility room in the back of the building was only about 32°. What bad timing to have trouble starting the generator. We did get it going, finally, and the room warmed quickly. We filled two tubs of rinse water from our ice-filled water tank.

My fingers were so numb that I could hardly hang the clothes up by the time I had rinsed each batch of clothes in two ice-cold tubs. Next time it's this cold I'm going to fill the rinse tubs the night before, so they will have time to warm a little.

It is now 2:30 p.m., and the sun has set already. There is an orange glow behind the mountains to the south. The days are slowly getting longer—about five minutes a day.

Last night, Tod set a broken leg—or, I should say, put a plaster cast on it, as only a doctor can set it. I don't know if we are going to be able to get this fellow out to a hospital in Nome. The dogsled trip is rough, probably too rough for someone with a broken leg. Last winter, we had two broken wrists and were able to get the patients out to the hospital, but it was easier for them to travel. We will discuss this case with the doctor in Kotzebue on the short-wave radio tonight.

We are going to have more company. Grace's supervisor, Gertrude Kunz, is visiting from Anchorage. She and Grace plan to come over to Savoonga for about a week. Because the nurse's quarters aren't finished, they'll be staying with us. Then, when they return to Gambell, Doctor Schiller from the Arctic Health Center in Anchorage will arrive. I must get the house cleaned.

I will send this letter back to Gambell with Grace, so it will be sure to go out on the next plane.

Love, Doris

❖ ❖ ❖

Sunday, February 20, 1954

Dear Mother,

Tod has been asked by the ANS office in Juneau to organize a reindeer count on St. Lawrence Island and has been promised funds for the undertaking. He'll probably travel around the island by dogsled for about a week in April.

We've been so lucky this year with the weather—almost no wind to speak of since the big blow during the measles epidemic. A few weeks ago, we did have a short spell of two to three days of 50-mile-an-hour winds and low temperatures of about -20. Aside from that, the winter was mild (relatively to subarctic winters on the mainland) with temperatures hovering between 0 and -20°.

As I write this, I am watching several dogsled teams bring us blocks of ice from the lake. The unseasonably warm weather makes it possible for the villagers to cut the ice, which is usually too thick to cut at this time of year.

Everyone is speculating whether the Coast Guard cutter will stop at Savoonga soon. It was in Nome a week or so ago, and we heard indirectly that it had been to King Island. Its movements are kept secret, so we don't know if or when it might come. The floe ice isn't thick, and the villagers are certain the ship can break through the ice to get in. We hope so. The cutter will have a doctor, and we might have an opportunity to come aboard for dinner and perhaps see a movie.

I just finished *From Here to Eternity* by James Jones and thoroughly enjoyed it. We are eager to see the movie that was released last year starring Burt Lancaster and Deborah Kerr. I imagine the story was censored extensively, but we hear the movie is a strong contender for an Academy Award.

Alice returned the second volume of Churchill's history of the war. She says she will concentrate on reading our books until she leaves this summer on a sabbatical.

I'm learning to speak a little Yupik. Some of the third-grade girls, my pets, suddenly have become uninhibited and are teaching me their Yupik names and other words. I've found that trying to learn their language is an effective way to get them to speak English, as they jabber away in English to make me understand Yupik.

We are enjoying reliable mail service again. The plane landed in Gambell yesterday about noon. Our dog teams left at 2 p.m. and returned to Savoonga around 10:30. Your letter dated February 15 was received in five days! Pretty good, eh?

Guess I'll close for now and look at the newly arrived magazines.

Love, Doris and Tod

❖ ❖ ❖

GAMBELL
Friday, March 4, 1954

Dear Mother,

I traveled to Gambell by dogsled yesterday with Clarence Pungowiyi. We had a smooth trip, covering 60 miles in seven hours—good time.

Just before we arrived, a heavy wind and rainstorm blew up—the first major storm since November. It is still raging today. I sure hope the weather improves before we return to Savoonga tomorrow.

I am staying with Grace. She has lovely new quarters, probably the nicest on the Island.

Having fresh eggs and meat here was a treat. I wish I could take something back for Tod. He sorely misses fresh eggs. But he will be happy if the steaks we ordered come on the next plane, as expected.

Tod is planning to go on a reindeer count for about a week in April. We decided this would be a good time for an outing to Gambell. I have never traveled cross-country by dogsled. This was my spring vacation, I guess.

Love, Doris

P.S. Grace plans to buy 12 cans of Coors beer at the Air Force station that I will smuggle back to Savoonga in the bottom of my sleeping bag. What a surprise and treat it will be for Tod!

❖ ❖ ❖

Monday, April 19, 1954

Dear Mother,

Tod got in from his reindeer count about 1:30 this morning. I was so glad to see him. He brought me this stationery from the Air Force station at Northeast Cape. I'll have to hurry and use it before we leave.

It was close to 3 a.m. by the time Tod got warm and had eaten. Then we visited for about an hour. Tod told me they did not see a single reindeer!

Tod is not teaching today as he still has a bad cold. He had just about licked it until his reindeer trip. It didn't help that he had to sleep outside on the snow one night in a sleeping bag.

Tod has arranged for us to leave the island on a military plane this spring from Northeast Cape, so it appears we won't have to wait for ice-free water to make a skinboat trip to fly out of Gambell. And we won't have to wait for the *North Star*, either.

I worked on various school reports while Tod was gone and have finished everything except the village census and our inventory. The inventory is almost complete, but I want Tod to check a few things before I type the final draft. Only four weeks left!

No more news. More later.

Love, Doris

❖ ❖ ❖

Tuesday, May 3, 1954

Dearest Mother,

Hunting started again today. All the shore ice is gone. This is rare, as the shore ice doesn't usually break off until around the first of June. The floe ice has receded far to the north, so there is much open water.

John Waghiyi, our postmaster, said the mail carrier is thinking of taking our mail to Gambell by skinboat rather than by dogsled. Good choice, evidently. The snow is melting fast. The blocks of ice we melt for water have been gone for quite a while, and we have been melting snow instead.

We may not have to teach beyond the end of May. Hunting hasn't disrupted our class time too much yet, so we should get our 180 days in unless hunting is exceptional, and the children are needed to help.

The days are getting long. We've become old fogies about our sleeping habits. We go to bed about 10 every night. Tod usually takes a nap after dinner. Sometimes he wakes up just in time to go to bed again. We really don't need the amount of sleep that we're getting, but we have little to do in the evenings. That's the boredom we told you about.

We have learned another plane is coming to Gambell on Friday. We had heard last week that no more mail planes were scheduled, as Alaska Airlines had fulfilled its contract. But tonight, on our short-wave call with the ANS office in Nome, Mr. Williams told us that the airline had agreed to make one more flight on May 7. We are happy to hear this good news as we haven't received mail for three weeks and we have some important mail to get out.

Well, I don't have any news.

Lots of love, Doris

❖ ❖ ❖

Monday, May 24, 1954

Dear Mother,

We finished school May 14. Hunting was going full force, and our attendance was low. Since then, however, a west wind has blown a lot of loose ice in close to shore, and hunting has been limited.

The walruses are moving north. The teacher on Little Diomede said they were pouring through the Bering Strait. We hope enough ice will break from the floe for the villagers to get in some more hunting soon. We have a little shore ice now, but the wind is making big waves and the men aren't hunting today.

I have been packing, cleaning, washing, and so forth. We still don't know exactly when we'll be able to leave. It won't be before June 4 at the earliest and it may be later, depending on when the ice clears at the east end of the Island. There is a lot of packing that I can't do until we are ready to leave.

I gave my red coat with the fur collar to Mary Pungowiyi, Helen and Clarence's daughter. She is a pretty girl about 17 who may be going out to school in a couple of years. The coat was well worn and too small for me. But it looked attractive on her. I'm going to give her some more clothes before we go.

The Pungowiyi children are so smart and handsome. The little girl, Lynn, is 10. She is one of my pets. Tod and I both adore her. Almost every day since school ended, Lynn and a couple of her friends have come to our quarters offering to help. I don't have much for them to do but greatly enjoy their company.

One day, the girls hung my curtains out on the line while I was washing. They asked when I would take them down and said they'd be back to do it. Lynn always speaks for everyone. Her English is nearly flawless. I wish we could take her with us!

Tod is proud of himself, and I am proud of him, too. He got our pump working this morning and is pumping water from the creek into our tank. This is a relief because most of the snow has melted, and our water supply is running low. Now we will be able to take baths in the tub. Tod is planning to heat lots of water for a bath tonight. I may wait until tomorrow. I'm not as dirty as Tod!

Did I tell you I am learning shorthand? I sent for a correspondence course in speedwriting advertised in a magazine. It is an easy method, based on letters of the alphabet instead of odd symbols. I work on a lesson every day and already can complete speed tests at 90 words a minute. I am on lesson 13. There are 25 basic lessons covering the principles. At some point, Tod will read a book of dictation to me. I hope to complete the course before we leave.

I was given a beautiful pair of earrings the other day by Albert Kulowiyi. Tod had given him a pair of shoes. So, the next day Albert brought me the earrings, which were made by his 12-year-old son, Alvin, who is another one of my pets. Albert is so proud of his son. Alvin is just like his father—precise and hardworking. I made a *faux pas* when I asked Albert to thank Alvin for the earrings. Albert explained that he had *paid* Alvin for making them.

Several touching conversations have taken place recently when villagers get onto the subject of our imminent departure. Jimmie Toolie suggested that we stay two more years and then go. He said, "Five years isn't too long!" I guess he didn't want to extend a blanket invitation for us to stay indefinitely, but it was alright to stay two more years. We were moved by his desire for us to stay.

Clarence Pungowiyi asked Tod yesterday what we were going to do next year. Tod told him about going back to school. Clarence then wanted to know what we would do after that. When Tod said he wasn't sure, Clarence suggested we should come back to Savoonga to teach again. It makes us feel good and a little sad, too, that some of the villagers are sorry that we are leaving and want us to come back.

This afternoon, I will pack a box of rugs and curtains that we are taking to New York and then start on the blankets and bedding.

Well, time for lunch, so will close for now. There is no chance of this letter getting off the Island before we go, so I'll mail it from Nome.

See you soon.

Love, Tod and Doris

Epilogue

✦ ✦ ✦

We left Savoonga on a spring day in early June 1954 just as we had come three years earlier—by skinboat on the windy Bering Sea. In the end, our departure was hastened by the powerful forces of nature that regulate so much of life at the edge of America.

Around noon, we received word that the floe ice had moved far enough away from the north coast so that we could sneak through safely with Jimmie Toolie and his skinboat crew to the Air Force station at Northeast Cape. But conditions could change at any time, so we had to move quickly.

▲ *Our last view of Savoonga as we left the village in June 1954 after teaching there three years.*

We had said our goodbyes throughout the village. Our farewell to Alice Green as we climbed into the skinboat was not the last time we saw her.[17]

As Savoonga receded into the distance, we reflected on how our response to that BIA telegram three years before had set our careers in motion. We had learned so much about the villagers' arduous, yet close-knit, mutually cooperative lives. We had come to admire greatly a generous and caring people who took us in like family. I knew we would miss our friends here even as we looked forward to our next adventure. The profound effects of teaching in a

⏶ *Pushing skinboat through the ice to shore near the Air Force station.*

remote village on the Bering Sea would influence the rest of our lives.

At the cape, we encountered remnants of the ice floe blocking us from landing. The men had to climb out and walk the heavy skinboat to shore through floating ice chunks—a task that took an hour or so. Fortunately, Tod was wearing his rubber boots.

⏶ *Northwest Cape Air Force Station*

By the time we had landed and unloaded our gear, it was too late to hike over to the Air Force station. So, we paused to have something to eat. Tod and I had brought surplus K-rations left over from the war that ANS had sent to the school for emergency use. Jimmy and his crew had their dried seal meat. We bedded down in Jimmie's trapping cabin for the night. Tod and I shared a sleeping bag—how COZY!

In the morning, we trekked over to the station. Two days later, we caught a ride on a military plane to Nome. From there, we took commercial flights to Seattle and points east, visiting our families on the way to New York.

Little did we know, as we waved goodbye to Savoonga, that we would return many years later.

❖ ❖ ❖

17. Alice left Savoonga in 1955. She served as the religious coordinator at the Alaska Native Medical Center in Anchorage until 1970. Two years later, she became the first woman in Alaska to be ordained as a Presbyterian minister. Alice then returned to Savoonga where she served as minister until 1982 when church rules forced her to retire at age 65. She visited us in New York and Fairbanks over the years and remained a life-long friend. Alice died in the Alaska Pioneers Home in Anchorage in December 2020. She was 103.

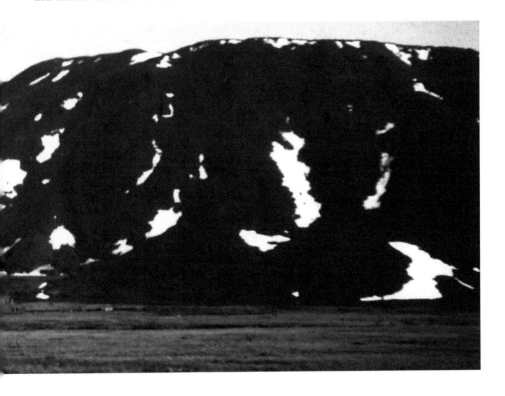

As planned, Tod earned a graduate degree at Columbia University. We expected to spend only a year in New York. However, one year stretched into three as he pursued doctoral studies.

In the spring of 1957, near the end of our third year, Tod was offered a professorship at the University of Alaska in Fairbanks that included a research grant from the U. S. Office of Education to undertake a comprehensive survey of native education throughout the Territory.

We returned to Alaska and settled down in Fairbanks, Tod at the university and I teaching advanced-placement history and government at Lathrop High School and later at West Valley High School. Over the years our careers progressed, and we became staunch citizens of Alaska.

In the spring of 1983, Tod was invited to Savoonga to give a commencement address to the first high school class graduating from the newly constructed school that now included grades K-12, an invitation he was delighted to accept (as was I).

More than 30 years after leaving the village, the Alaska we came to as young teachers had seen big changes. The Territory became a state in 1959. A major oil discovery was made at Prudhoe Bay on the Arctic Slope in 1968. Before the oil could be moved across Alaska through a pipeline to an ice-free port at Valdez on the southcentral coast, native land claims to sizeable portions of the state had to be settled.

Consequently, Congress passed the Alaska Native Claims Settlement Act of 1971. The villages of Savoonga and Gambell received title to more than one million acres of land on the island. After oil began flowing, tax revenue enabled the state to build modern new schools in many small communities throughout Alaska, including Savoonga, where operation of the BIA school had been transferred to the state.

We returned to a community far different from the one we left in 1954. No dogsled or skinboat transportation for us! We flew from Nome directly to Savoonga, which by then had daily air service and timely mail delivery.

Savoonga had grown with many new houses and larger buildings. The store had changed from a one-room building with limited products to a large self-service supermarket that included a frozen-food section, fresh produce, and almost anything that could be eaten, worn, or otherwise used.

We were taken from the airport to the principal's home on a snowmobile driven by our old friend, Jonathan Annogiyuk.

The principal and his wife told us they planned a get-together that evening with the teaching staff, which had been expanded considerably, to watch a football game on TV. Would we care to join them? We declined with thanks, wanting to spend our limited time visiting old friends in the village.

▲ Top and middle: An aerial view of Savoonga in 1983 when we traveled to the village by air for the first time ever. ▲ Above: Jonathan Annogiyuk showed us one of the three-wheelers that were replacing the dogsleds.

In conversations with a few teachers, we inquired about several local families and learned the teachers had little knowledge about what went on in the community. The new school was constructed in a large open area between the village and the old school, which had been converted into teacher housing. This created a large physical barrier. Apparently, the teachers were content to live their lives on their side of the barrier. This surprised us. Tod and I had been in and out of peoples' homes every day and were active participants in village life.

I met old friend Janet Kingeekuk in the laundromat and found one of my little first-graders, Dorcas Kulowiyi, running the village library. Other new buildings included a clinic and several government offices. Telephone and service had become available. Thanks to satellite technology, residents of the once remote, isolated village could call anywhere in the world.

▲ ▲ *I discovered one of my students, Dorcas Kulowiyi, was the village librarian.*
▲ *Savoonga's first class of high school graduates received their degrees in the new school.*

▲ ▲ Left to right: I found Janet Kingeekuk, an old friend, at the laundromat; the class president presented Tod with a gift from the community, an exquisite ivory carving. ▲ We met Dean and Gloria Kulowiyi, Tod's former students, and their baby.

One particularly touching moment came when our old friend Katherine Noongwook came to visit, bringing a young woman with her. She told us, "This is the baby whose life you saved from measles." We were delighted to see her though sorry to learn that the disease had left her with diminished hearing.

We also became reacquainted on the flight from Nome with Caleb Pungowiyi, whom I taught in third grade. By then in his late 30s, Caleb had become a widely respected activist in native affairs and a leader in one of the native corporations created in the land claims settlement. Like Tod, he had been invited to speak to the graduates.

In his address, Caleb spoke about the school. In words I am paraphrasing, he told them, "You have been fortunate to study in this beautiful new this building and to have educational opportunities in facilities such as these, which were

▲ *Summer sunset*

unavailable to me and my classmates as we grew up. However, we had something that was more important. We had teachers such as Tod and Doris Ray, who believed in us and cared about us. We were the fortunate ones!"

These words brought tears to my eyes. They still do.

❖ ❖ ❖

Despite a prediction in 1952 from the Scandinavian captain of the *North Star* that pressure on our marriage in a remote village with few non-natives might result in our leaving Savoonga in "separate skinboats," Tod and I were married for more than 68 years until his death in 2020.

Bibliography

❖ ❖ ❖

Introduction

"G.I. Bill," *Wikipedia*, accessed July 30, 2022. https://en.m.wikipedia.org/wiki/G.I. Bill

Native Words, Native Warriors, "Struggling with Cultural Repression," National Museum of the American Indian, Smithsonian Institute, accessed July 30, 2022. https://americanindian.si.edu/nk360/code-talkers/boarding-schools/

Section 1

"We are the Salmon People," Columbia River Inter-Tribal Fish Commission, accessed July 31, 2022, https://CRITFC.org

Native Education

Ray, Charles K, *A Program of Education for Alaskan Natives*, Revised Edition. Fairbanks: University of Alaska, 1959.

"Sheldon Jackson," Alaskaweb.org. www.alaskaweb.org/bios/jacksonsheldon.html

Haycox, Stephen W., "Sheldon Jackson in Historical Perspective-Alaska Natives and Mission Contracts, 1885-1894, *The Pacific Historian*, Vol. XXVIII, No.1: 18-28. www.alaskool.org/native_ed/articles/s_haycox/sheldon_jackson.htm

"Rev. Sheldon Jackson, Alaska's First General Agent for Education, 1834-1909," Alaska State Museum: Community Life/Education, University of Alaska Fairbanks.

"Early Education and Effects of the Nelson Act (1905)," Department of Tribal governance, University of Alaska Fairbanks. https://uaf.edu/tribal/academics/112/unit-2earlyeducation andeffectsofthenelsonact1905.php

North Star

Burg, Amos, "North Star Cruises Alaska's Wild West," *National Geographic*, 57-86, July 1952.

Making a Walrus Skinboat

Neme, Laurel, "Making Walrus Skin Boats," laurelneme.com https://www.laurelneme.com/making-walrus-skin-boats/

Cold War

Scrudato, R.J.; Chiarenzelli, Jeff; Miller, Pamela; Clark R. Alexander, Jr. and others. "Contaminants at Arctic formerly used defense sites": *Journal of Local and Global Health Science*; November 2012(1):2. DOI:10.5339/jlghs.2012.2

Garrett, Wilber E. and Steve Raymer, "Air Bridge to Siberia," National Geographic, v. 147. October 1988, pp. 504-509.

Ice Floes/Walruses

Demuth, Bathsheba. "The Walrus and the Bureaucrat: Energy, Ecology, and Making the State in the Russian and American Arctic, 1870–1950": *The American Historical Review*, Vol. 124, Issue 2, April 2019: 483–510.
https://academic.oup.com/ahr/article/124/2/483/5426289

Fay, F.H.; Eberhardt, E.B.; Kelly, B.P.; Burns, J.J.; and Quakenbush, L.T.; "Status of the Pacific Walrus Population, 1950-1989": *Marine Mammal Science*, 13(4):537-565, October 1997).

"Eskimo Walrus Commission," Kawerak, Inc.
https://kawerak.org/natural-resources/eskimo-walrus-commission/

Pease, Carol H.; Schoenberg, Sally A.; and Overland, James E.; "A Climatology of the Bering Sea and Its Relation to Sea Ice Extent": *NOAA Technical Report* ERL 419-PMEL 36: 3-4, March 1982, Pacific Management Environmental Laboratory: Seattle, Wash.

Reindeer

"Savoonga," Aleut International Association; the Community Observation Network for Adaptation and Security (CONAS).
https://conas-ak.org/conas-community/savoonga-alaska/

Bucki, Carrie, "Reindeer Roundup", "Reindeer History in Alaska," Reindeer Research Program, University of Alaska Fairbanks, 2004.

Haecker, Diana, "Reindeer Herding Holds Great Future for Seward Peninsula," *Nome Nugget*, August 12, 2010, reprinted by Alaska Department of Fish and Game.

"Reindeer Herders Association," Kawerak Inc.
https://kawerak.org/natural-resources/reindeer-herders-association/

Lincoln, Amber; Lotvonen, Varpu; Plattet, Patrick, and the British Museum, "Frank Churchill's 1905 Documentation of the Reindeer Service in Alaska Bering Land Bridge National Preserve," *Alaska Park Science*, Vol. 20, Issue 2, National Park Service. https://www.nps.gov/articles/000/aps-20-2-5.htm

Epilogue

Khachatoorian, Travis; "Million-acre St. Lawrence Island land title signed over to native population," KTTU; July 28, 2016.

About the Author

* * *

"Virgil" Violet

▲ Doris D. Ray

"Billy" Begonia

Born in 1927 to parents who had emigrated from Canada, Doris D. Ray grew up and was educated in Detroit. After graduation from college and earning a Master of Arts degree, she moved to the University of Colorado to engage in doctoral studies in Slavic history while teaching a course in western civilization.

She met her future husband, Charles "Tod" Ray, a World War II veteran, who was a student at the university. They married after Tod's graduation, then left Colorado for St. Lawrence Island in the northern Bering Sea, where they taught school for three years.

After teaching in Savoonga, Tod and Doris took a giant step across the continent into a whole new culture to pursue graduate studies at Columbia University in New York City.

They returned to Alaska after several years in New York—Tod to the University of Alaska and Doris to the Fairbanks public schools where she taught advanced-placement history and political science and served as high school social studies department head and later as director of secondary education for the school district. She also served on numerous state and national educational commissions and boards.

Following their retirement, Doris and Tod moved to Seattle and continued their travels throughout the world, visiting every continent except Antarctica. As Doris pointed out, "No need to go to Antarctica when I've lived most of my life in subarctic Alaska and have spent time in Point Barrow at the top of the world. I'll just visit the penguins in the zoo."